JAMESTOWN  EDUCATION

English, Yes!

Learning English Through Literature

Level 7: Transitional

 Glencoe

New York, New York   Columbus, Ohio   Chicago, Illinois   Peoria, Illinois   Woodland Hills, California

JAMESTOWN EDUCATION

Cover photo illustration: Third Eye Image/Solus Photography/Veer.

Send all inquiries to:
Glencoe/McGraw-Hill
8787 Orion Place
Columbus, OH 43240-4027

ISBN 0-07-860025-1
Printed in the United States of America.
1 2 3 4 5 6 7 8 9 10 021 08 07 06 05 04 03

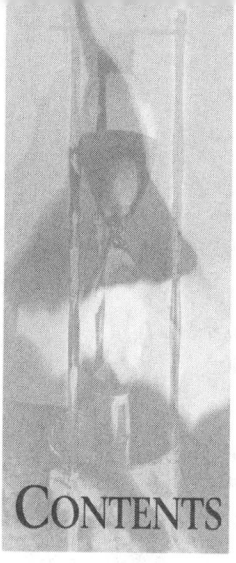

CONTENTS

Unit 1: The Teacher 1
by Alma Flor Ada

Unit 2: The Tiger. 19
based on a story by Lin Yutang

       Magic Words (poem) 26
       by a Netsilik Inuit

Unit 3: After Twenty Years 41
based on a story by O. Henry

Unit 4: The Stove 57
based on a story by Marjorie Pickthall

Unit 5: Early Autumn 81

       The City (poem) 85

       Lonely House (song lyrics) 86

       Declaration (poem) 87

       Dreams (poem) 88
       by Langston Hughes

Unit 6: An Occurrence at Owl Creek Bridge 103
based on a story by Ambrose Bierce

Unit 7: Ta-Na-E-Ka 123
         based on a story by Mary Whitebird

         Grandfather (poem) 133
         by James K. Cazalas

Unit 8: The Circuit 147
         based on a story by Francisco Jiménez

Unit 9: A Boy's Best Friend 167
         based on a story by Isaac Asimov

         Moco Limping (poem) 172
         by David Nava Monreal

Score Chart 184

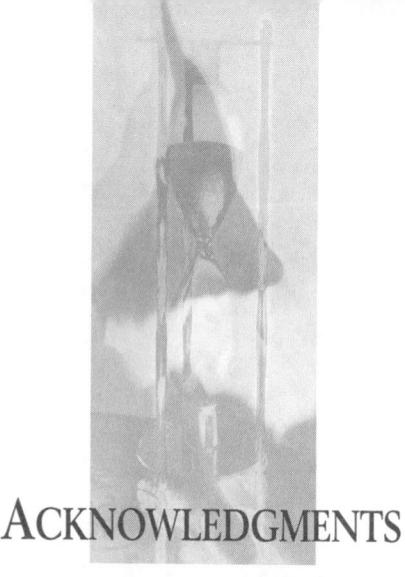

ACKNOWLEDGMENTS

Acknowledgment is gratefully made to the following publishers, authors, and agents for permission to reprint these works. Every effort has been made to determine copyright owners. In the case of any omissions, the Publisher will be pleased to make suitable acknowledgments in future editions. Adaptations and/or abridgments are by Burton Goodman.

"The Teacher." Reprinted and recorded with the permission of Atheneum Books for Young Readers, an imprint of Simon & Schuster Children's Publishing Division, from *Where the Flame Trees Bloom* by Alma Flor Ada. Text copyright © 1994 Alma Flor Ada.

"The Tiger." From *Famous Chinese Short Stories* by Lin Yutang. Copyright © 1948, 1951, 1952 by (John Day Company) Harper & Row, Publishers, Inc. Reprinted by permission of the estate of Lin Yutang.

"Early Autumn" from *Something in Common* by Langston Hughes. Copyright © 1963 by Langston Hughes. Copyright renewed © 1991 by Arnold Rampersad and Ramona Bass. Reprinted by permission of Hill & Wang, a division of Farrar, Straus & Giroux, Inc.

"The City," "Declaration," and "Dreams" from *Collected Poems* by Langston Hughes. Copyright © 1994 by the Estate of Langston Hughes. Reprinted by permission of Alfred A. Knopf Inc.

"Lonely House" from the musical *Street Scene,* score by Kurt Weill. Copyright © 1946 by Kurt Weill and Langston Hughes. Reprinted by permission of Warner/Chappell, Inc.

"Ta-Na-E-Ka" by Mary Whitebird. Copyright © 1972, 1973 by Scholastic Magazines. Reprinted by permission of Scholastic Inc.

"Grandfather" by James K. Cazalas. All attempts have been made to locate the copyright holder.

"The Circuit" by Francisco Jiménez, from *Arizona Quarterly,* Autumn 1973. Copyright Arizona Board of Regents. Reprinted by permission of Arizona Board of Regents.

"A Boy's Best Friend" by Isaac Asimov, from *Boys' Life,* March 1975. Copyright © 1975 by the Boy Scouts of America, published by permission of The Estate of Isaac Asimov, c/o Ralph M. Vicinanza, Ltd.

"Moco Limping" by David Nava Monreal. Reprinted by permission of the author.

JAMESTOWN EDUCATION

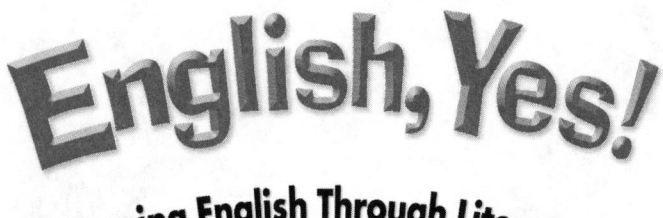

English, Yes!

Learning English Through Literature

Level 7: Transitional

THE TEACHER

by Alma Flor Ada

Connections

Read the title and study the picture on the left. Describe what you see.

- Where do you think this story takes place?
- Which person in the picture is the teacher? How do you know?
- Why do you think the class is being held outside?
- Who do you think the man is?
- Would you enjoy having classes outdoors? Why or why not?

As you read, think about how the picture connects to the story.

Words to Learn

In this story, you will learn some new words. You will also learn some idioms. For example, *brought up* is an idiom that means "watched over and helped grow."

THE TEACHER

by Alma Flor Ada

Life was her classroom.

My mother's mother, my grandmother Dolores, was known as
Lola. She filled my early years with outdoor adventures, fun, and
fascinating stories. The deeds of the Greek gods and goddesses, the
heroic acts of the Cuban patriots, were as immediate to me as her
everyday life at the two schools where she was principal: an
elementary public school during the day and a school for working
women in the evenings.

It is not surprising that there are many stories in our family
about this woman who was both an intellectual and a practical
person, who cut her hair and shortened her skirts before any other
woman in our town, who created a literary journal, set up schools,
awakened a great passion in the poet who married her, and brought
up five children as well as several nieces and nephews while
directing her own schools and farm.

One of my favorite stories about her was told to me at various
times by my mother and by my aunts Mireya and Virginia, since
all three of them were present when the events took place. Unlike
many other family stories, which are often changed or embellished
depending on the teller, I have always heard this story told exactly
the same way. Perhaps that is because the story itself is too powerful
to be embellished, or because the events impressed themselves so
vividly upon the memories of those present.

My grandmother Lola loved to teach outdoors. The slightest
reason would serve to take the whole class out under the trees to
conduct her lessons there. This particular story took place during
one of those outdoor lessons, at a time when she and her husband,

my grandfather Medardo, ran a boarding school on the hacienda[1] she had inherited from her father and where later I would be born.

Surrounded by her pupils, including three of her own daughters, my grandmother was conducting a grammar lesson. Suddenly she interrupted herself. "Why is it," she asked her students, "that we don't often speak about the things that are truly important? About our responsibility as human beings for those around us? Do we really know their feelings, their needs? And yet we could all do so much for each other. . . ."

The students were silent, fascinated. They knew their teacher sometimes strayed[2] from the topic of the lesson in order to share with them her own reflections. And they also knew that those were some of her most important lessons. At times she could be funny and witty. Other times, she would touch their hearts. And so they listened.

1. *hacienda:* a large ranch.
2. *strayed:* wandered away.

"Look," continued my grandmother, as she pointed to the road that bordered the farm. There the students saw a solitary man walking. "Look at that old man. He is walking by us. In a few minutes he will be gone forever, and we will never have known who he is, where he is going, what may be important in his life."

The students watched the man, who by then was quite close. He was very thin, and a coarse *guayabera*[3] hung loosely over his bent frame. His face, in the shade of a straw hat, was tired and wrinkled.

"Well," said my grandmother, "do we let him go away, forever unknown, or do you want to ask him if there is anything we can do for him?"

The students looked at one another. Finally one girl said, "Shall I ask him?" As my grandmother nodded, the girl got up and walked toward the road. A few of the other students followed her, my mother and my aunts among them.

Upon seeing them approach, the man stopped. "We would like to know who you are, and where you are going," said the student. "Is there anything we can do for you?" added my aunt Mireya.

The man was completely shocked. "But, who are *you*?" was all he could reply.

The girls then explained how their questions had come about. The old man looked at them. He told them that he had no one to be with, that he had come a long distance hoping to find some distant relatives, but had been unable to locate them. "I'm nothing but an old man," he concluded, "looking for a place to lie down and die. As a matter of fact, I was heading toward that large *ceiba*." He pointed to a large tree growing by the road not too far away. "I thought I'd lie down in its shade to wait for my death."

"Please don't leave" was all the girls could say. They rushed back to tell their teacher what they had learned from the old man, that he truly intended to just lie down and die.

"What do you think can be done?" my grandmother asked. The boys and girls came up with ideas: The old man could go to an old folks' home. Maybe he should be taken to the hospital, or perhaps

3. *guayabera:* a loose-fitting shirt.

the police would know what to do. . . . "Is that what you would like to happen, if it were you?" my grandmother asked.

Instead, the children took the man into the house. He was given a room. The students made the bed and cooked him some food. A doctor determined that there was nothing wrong with him except exhaustion and malnutrition. It took him several days to recuperate, but soon he was up and about. He lived on with the family for many years, until one morning he was found to have died peacefully in his sleep. During all those years, he helped in the garden, fed the hens, or often sat on the back porch, whistling softly. But there was nothing he liked better than to sit in the back of the classroom or out under the trees and listen to my grandmother teach.

Meet the Author

Alma Flor Ada *(born 1938)* grew up in Cuba and lived in Spain and Peru before moving to California, where she now lives. She is the author of many popular children's books and mystery novels for young adults. Ada is the director of the Center for Multicultural Literature for Children and Young Adults at the University of San Francisco. She is also president of the International Association for Children's Literature in Spanish and Portuguese. "The Teacher" appears in one of her best-known books, *Where the Flame Trees Bloom*. Her other works include *The Wall's Dwarf and Other Tales* and *The Ladybug's Dots and Other Stories*.

Put an *x* in the box next to the correct answer.

Reading Comprehension

1. The author's grandmother was
   - ❏ **a.** a doctor.
   - ❏ **b.** a lawyer.
   - ❏ **c.** a principal.

2. Grandmother Lola loved to
   - ❏ **a.** teach outdoors.
   - ❏ **b.** watch television.
   - ❏ **c.** play baseball and other sports.

3. Which expression best describes the old man who was walking nearby?
   - ❏ **a.** young and vigorous
   - ❏ **b.** old and thin
   - ❏ **c.** smiling and joyful

4. The man said that he was looking for
   - ❏ **a.** his son.
   - ❏ **b.** his wife.
   - ❏ **c.** a place to die.

5. Where did the children take the man?
   - ❏ **a.** into the house
   - ❏ **b.** to a hospital
   - ❏ **c.** to the police

6. What did the man like to do most?
   - ❏ **a.** work in the garden
   - ❏ **b.** feed the hens
   - ❏ **c.** listen to Lola teach

Vocabulary

7. The students saw nothing but a solitary man walking along a road. The word *solitary* means
   - ❏ **a.** lone.
   - ❏ **b.** heavy.
   - ❏ **c.** smart.

8. The man had walked for a long time and was suffering from exhaustion. Someone who is suffering from *exhaustion* is
   - ❏ **a.** out of work.
   - ❏ **b.** very tired.
   - ❏ **c.** very poor.

9. The teacher liked to share her reflections with the students. As used here, the word *reflections* means
   - ❏ **a.** food.
   - ❏ **b.** thoughts.
   - ❏ **c.** faces in a mirror.

Idioms

10. Grandmother Lola brought up five children and several nieces and nephews. The idiom *brought up* means
    - ❏ **a.** pulled along.
    - ❏ **b.** sent to many schools.
    - ❏ **c.** watched over and helped grow.

How many questions did you answer correctly? Circle your score. Then fill in your score on the Score Chart on page 184.

Number Correct	1	2	3	4	5	6	7	8	9	10
Score	10	20	30	40	50	60	70	80	90	100

EXERCISES TO HELP YOU

Exercise A

Understanding the story. Answer each question by writing a complete sentence. Be sure your sentences are grammatically correct. You may look back at the story.

1. Where did Grandmother Lola work as a principal during the day?

   _____

   _____

2. Where did she work as a principal in the evenings?

   _____

   _____

3. Describe the face of the old man who was walking by.

   _____

   _____

4. What did a student ask the man?

   _____

   _____

5. Whom was the man looking for?

   _____

   _____

6. What was the man planning to do?

   _____

   _____

7. What did the doctor say about the man?

_____

_____

_____

8. How long did the man live with the family?

_____

_____

9. How did the man help the family?

_____

_____

10. What did the man like to do most?

_____

_____

Exercise B

Adding vocabulary. On the left are 10 words from the story. Complete each sentence by adding the correct word. The first one has been done for you.

wrinkled

responsibility

concluded

inherited

patriots

slightest

malnutrition

intellectual

fascinating

conducting

1. Since Grandmother Lola's stories were filled with adventure, the children found them _____*fascinating*_____.

2. She sometimes taught at a ranch that she had _____ from her father.

3. Grandmother Lola believed that human beings should accept _____ for one another.

4. She loved to teach outdoors. Whenever she had the _____ reason, she took the class outside.

5. Grandmother Lola read many books and wrote stories and poems. She was a very _____ person.

6. The children heard tales about the courage of the Cuban _____.

7. One afternoon, Grandmother Lola was _____ a lesson in grammar.

8. They saw a man whose face was tired and _____.

9. Since he was suffering from _____, they gave him some food.

10. "I am nothing but an old man," he _____.

Exercise C

Part A

Putting events in order from random notes. Write a complete sentence for each group of words. Add capital letters, periods, and the appropriate words. Write the completed sentences on the lines. Then put the events in the order in which they occurred. You may look back at the story. The first one has been done for you.

1. _c_　　**a.** looking for a place to die

_____

_____

_____

2. ____　　**b.** recovered and lived happily

_____

_____

_____

3. ____　　**c.** Grandmother Lola teaching a class

One day Grandmother Lola was teaching

_a class outdoors._____

_____

4. ____　　**d.** an old man walking by

_____

_____

_____

5. ____　　**e.** took the old man into the house and

_____

_____

_____

6. ____   **f.** asked the students if they wanted

_____

_____

_____

7. ____   **g.** student asked the man

_____

_____

Part B

Now **summarize** the story in a paragraph by writing the sentences in the correct order. The first sentence of the paragraph appears below.

One day Grandmother Lola was teaching a class outdoors.

_____

_____

_____

_____

_____

_____

_____

_____

_____

_____

_____

_____

Exercise D

Finding synonyms. Read the sentence. Then select the **synonym** (the word most similar in meaning) for the word in capital letters. Circle the letter of the correct answer. Each capitalized word appears in the story.

1. Grandmother Lola told the children about the deeds of the Greek gods and goddesses.

   DEEDS   **a.** actions   **b.** problems   **c.** homes

2. They never forgot the story; they remembered it vividly.

   VIVIDLY   **a.** poorly   **b.** clearly   **c.** happily

3. Lola was often serious, but she could be funny and witty.

   WITTY   **a.** sad   **b.** scared   **c.** amusing

4. They learned of the heroic acts of people who loved their country.

   HEROIC   **a.** easy   **b.** lucky   **c.** brave

5. Their teacher sometimes strayed from the lesson she was teaching.

   STRAYED   **a.** wandered   **b.** wrote   **c.** forgot

6. The topic of the lesson that day was grammar.

   TOPIC   **a.** test   **b.** subject   **c.** beginning

7. The old man said that he intended to lie down and die.

   INTENDED   **a.** planned   **b.** asked   **c.** rushed

8. He had been looking for some relatives, but he was unable to locate them.

   LOCATE   **a.** write   **b.** help   **c.** find

9. A doctor determined that the man needed food and rest.

   DETERMINED   **a.** hoped   **b.** decided   **c.** remembered

10. It took the man several days to recuperate, but soon he was walking around.

    RECUPERATE   **a.** recover   **b.** obey   **c.** wash

Exercise E

Understanding characters in a story. How well did you grasp the author's **characterization** (the way a character acts, looks, speaks, and thinks)? Fill in the box next to the correct answer.

1. Which expression best characterizes Grandmother Lola?
   - ❑ **a.** old, weak, and tired
   - ❑ **b.** intelligent, hardworking, and caring
   - ❑ **c.** boring and dull

2. When she was teaching a class, Lola
   - ❑ **a.** never discussed her thoughts about life.
   - ❑ **b.** sometimes used life, itself, as the subject of a lesson.
   - ❑ **c.** taught nothing but facts.

3. Lola believed that people should
   - ❑ **a.** mind their own business at all times.
   - ❑ **b.** think only about themselves.
   - ❑ **c.** try to help others.

4. Which did Lola enjoy most?
   - ❑ **a.** teaching and telling stories
   - ❑ **b.** punishing students who did poorly
   - ❑ **c.** listening to the radio

Characters sometimes change during the course of a story.

5. When the students first met the old man, he was
   - ❑ **a.** cheerful and friendly.
   - ❑ **b.** healthy and strong.
   - ❑ **c.** very sad and lonely.

6. During the time he spent with the family, the man was
   - ❑ **a.** very disappointed.
   - ❑ **b.** helpful and happy.
   - ❑ **c.** angry and confused.

Exercise F
Vocabulary review. Write a complete sentence for each word.

1. exhaustion _____

   _____

2. solitary _____

   _____

3. responsibility _____

   _____

4. malnutrition _____

   _____

5. deeds _____

   _____

6. vividly _____

   _____

7. heroic _____

   _____

8. inherited _____

   _____

9. recuperate _____

   _____

10. topic _____

    _____

Sharing with Others

This section has been designed to provide you with opportunities to share your thoughts and ideas with others, while you practice and improve your reading, writing, speaking, and listening skills.

Part A

Discuss the following questions. Share your answers with your partner or with the group.

1. Sometimes we say that a person is "ahead of her (or his) time." What does this mean? How was Grandmother Lola ahead of her time? Find specific examples from the story to support your answer.

2. Suppose that Lola had not called her students' attention to the old man who was walking by. What do you think would have happened to him?

3. Do you agree that life itself was Grandmother Lola's classroom? Explain.

4. Grandmother Lola was famous for her stories. They were told and retold by the members of her family. Do you have a favorite story, one that relates to yourself or to your family or country? If so, share the story.

5. Think of a teacher or some other adult who has influenced your life for the better. Tell about that person.

6. What lesson, or lessons, does "The Teacher" teach?

Part B

1. Grandmother Lola stated, "Why is it that we don't often speak about the things that are truly important? About our responsibility as human beings for those around us . . . we could all do so much for each other."

   Do you agree or disagree with Grandmother Lola that we all have responsibility for those around us? On the lines below, write a **paragraph** that explains your point of view. Begin the paragraph with a **topic sentence** (a sentence that gives the main idea of the paragraph).

   _____

   _____

   _____

   _____

   _____

   _____

   _____

   _____

   _____

   _____

   _____

   _____

2. Refer to question 5. On the lines below, describe someone who has been a positive influence upon your life.

_____

_____

_____

_____

_____

_____

_____

_____

_____

_____

_____

_____

_____

_____

THE TIGER

based on a story by Lin Yutang

Connections

Study the picture on the left. Describe what you see.

- Does this story take place in a city or in a rural area? What do the buildings look like?
- Are the men friends? What do you think they are doing?
- In what way do you think the tiger will be important in the story?
- Do you like stories about people and animals? Why or why not?

As you read, think about how the picture connects to the story.

Words to Learn

In this story, you will learn some new words. You will also learn an idiom. For example, *take a nap* is an idiom that means "sleep."

THE TIGER

based on a story by Lin Yutang

There stood the man who had killed his father.

Chang Feng was traveling in the southern part of China during the reign of Emperor Yuanho in the year 806. Chang lived in the north and had never been to that part of the country before, so everything was new and fascinating to him.

One day he stopped at an inn in the town of Hengsham. After he unpacked his luggage, he went out to take a walk. The countryside was very green and there was a refreshing breeze that came over the mountain. He strolled on and on, enjoying everything enormously. He felt strangely excited.

It was autumn, and the hillsides glowed with red and gold leaves from the trees. A beautiful white temple stood halfway up the mountain. As the sun began to set, the green and blue and purple colors of the fields mixed with the dazzling red and gold of the trees. It was like a magic land.

Suddenly Chang had a strange sensation. He felt weak. Stars danced before his eyes and he was dizzy. He thought it was due to the altitude, or from the exertion of having walked so much, or perhaps he was affected by the colors and the light.

A few feet in front of him, he saw a pasture that had a thick, soft lawn. He took off his jacket, put it on the grass, and lay down to rest. He felt a little better now. As he looked up at the blue sky, he thought how beautiful and peaceful nature was. Men fought for money and fame. They lied and cheated and killed for gain. But here was peace—in nature. As he lay on the grass, he felt happy and relaxed. The smell of the green grass and a gentle breeze soon put him to sleep.

When he woke up, he felt hungry and realized that it was late in

the day. As he rolled his hands over his stomach, he touched soft fur. Quickly he sat up and saw that his body was covered with beautiful black stripes. As he stretched his arms, he felt a delightful new strength in them, thick and full of power. He yawned and was surprised at his own powerful roar. Looking down at his own face, he saw the tips of long white whiskers. Suddenly he realized that he had been transformed into a tiger!

"Now that is delightful," he thought to himself. "I am no longer a man, but a tiger. It is not bad for a change."

Eager to try his new strength, he ran into the woods and bounced from rock to rock, delighted with his new strength. He went up to the temple and knocked at the door with his paw, seeking to be admitted.

"It is a tiger!" he heard a priest shouting inside. "Do not open the door!"

"Now that is too bad," he thought to himself. "I only wanted to have supper with him and talk for a while. But of course I am a tiger now, and I suppose that makes a difference."

He had an instinct that he should go down the hill to the village and seek food. As he hid behind a hedge on a country path, he saw a young woman passing by.

"I would like to talk to her," he said to himself. But as he started to move toward the woman, she screamed and ran for her life.

"What kind of life is this when everyone thinks you are an enemy?" he wondered. "I would not hurt her."

He continued to walk. But then he realized that he was hungry, very hungry. "I would like a nice fat pig, or a small juicy lamb," he thought to himself. When he thought this, his mouth watered, and he felt ashamed of himself. But there was this terrible hunger gnawing at his stomach, and he knew he had to eat something or die. He searched the village for a pig or calf or even a chicken. But they were all locked up. All doors were shut against him. As he crouched in a dark alley, waiting for some stray animal to wander by, he heard people talking inside their houses. They were talking about a tiger that was loose in the village.

Since there was no food to satisfy his hunger, he went back to the mountain. He lay in wait for something to come his way. All night he waited, but nothing came by. For a while he must have fallen asleep.

He woke up before dawn. Some travelers were beginning to walk along the mountain road. Just then he saw a man run up to the travelers.

"Have you seen Li Wen?" the man breathlessly asked the travelers.

"He was finishing breakfast when we left the inn," said one of the travelers. "He should be coming along in just a few minutes."

"I have been sent to meet him," said the man. "But I have never seen Li Wen before. Is he traveling alone, or is he accompanied by others? Please tell me what he is wearing, so that I will recognize him when he comes along."

"Well," said the traveler, "Li Wen is with two other men. There are three of them traveling together. Li Wen is the one who is dressed in dark green clothing."

As he listened to this conversation, something told the tiger that he must eat Li Wen. Just why he must eat that person he did not know. But he had a very strong feeling that Li Wen was destined to be his first victim. In fact, as the tiger listened to the conversation from his hiding place, it seemed as if it were taking place especially for his benefit. He had never seen or heard of Li Wen in his life and knew nothing about that individual. Still, he crouched in the tall grass and waited for his victim.

Soon he saw Li Wen coming up the road with two other companions. When Li Wen came close enough, the tiger, Chang, rushed out, knocked him to the ground, and carried him up the mountain. The travelers were so frightened that they all ran away. Chang's hunger was satisfied, and he only felt as if he had had a bigger breakfast than usual.

Satisfied with his meal, he lay down to take a nap. When he

woke up he thought he must have been crazy to eat a human being
who had done him no harm. "I must have been mad to do such a
thing," he said to himself. His head cleared and he decided it was
not such a pleasant life, prowling night after night for food. He
remembered the night before, when hunger drove him to the village
and up the mountain, and he could do nothing to stop himself.

"I shall go back to that lawn and see if I can become a human
being," he said to himself.

He found the place on the lawn where he had left his jacket.
Then he lay down on the lawn, wishing he might wake up and be a
man again. He rolled over on the grass and in a few seconds found
that he had been changed back to his human shape.

Chang Feng was delighted, but he was puzzled by the strange
experience. He put on his jacket and started back to the town. When
he reached the inn, he found that he had been gone for exactly
twenty-four hours.

"Where have you been?" asked the innkeeper. "We have been
searching for you all day. We were extremely worried about you.
There was a tiger in the area. He was seen by a woman in the village
last night, and this morning, a guest, Li Wen, was eaten by him. I am
relieved to see that you have returned here safely."

Chang Feng made up a story that he had spent the night in the
temple.

"You are very lucky!" exclaimed the innkeeper, shaking his
head. "It was in that vicinity that Li Wen was killed by the tiger."

"No, the tiger will not eat me," Chang Feng replied.

"Why not?"

"He cannot," Chang Feng said mysteriously.

Chang Feng kept the secret to himself, for he certainly could not reveal to anyone what had happened.

Chang Feng went back to his home in Honan, and several years went by. One day he went to Huaiyang, a city on the Huai River. His friends made a dinner party for him and much wine was consumed. Between the courses, the guests were each asked to tell about a strange experience.

Chang Feng began to tell his own story, and it happened that one of the guests was the son of Li Wen, the man he had eaten. As Chang went on with his story, the young man's face grew angrier and angrier.

"So it was *you* who killed my father!" the young man shouted at him furiously.

Chang Feng quickly stood up and apologized. He knew that he had gotten himself into a very serious situation. "I am sorry," said Chang. "I did not know that it was your father."

The young man suddenly picked up a knife from the table and threw it at Chang. Luckily, it missed and fell with a clang on the floor. The young man rushed at Chang, but the other guests grabbed the man and held him back.

"I will kill you to avenge my father's death! I will follow you to the ends of the earth!" the young man shouted.

The friends persuaded Chang Feng to leave the house at once and told him to hide for a while, while they tried to calm Li Wen's son. Everyone agreed that to avenge one's father's death was a noble thing. But after all, Chang Feng had eaten Li Wen when he was a tiger, and no one wanted to see more blood flow. It was an unusual situation and it raised a difficult question—whether revenge was right in this case under the circumstances. Still, the young man swore to kill Chang to avenge his father's death.

Finally the friends contacted the governor of the region. The governor ordered Li Wen's son to cross the Huai River and never to return. Chang Feng, on his part, changed his name and went to the northern part of the country to keep as far away from his enemy as possible.

When Li Wen's son returned to his home, his friends said to him, "We know how you feel, and we sympathize with you. We understand why you want revenge for your father's death. However,

Chang Feng ate your father when he was a tiger and is not responsible for his action. He did not know your father and had no reason to kill him. That was a strange and special case, but he did not plan to murder your father, and if you kill Chang Feng, *you* will be accused of murder yourself."

The son respected this advice and decided not to hunt down Chang Feng anymore.

Meet the Author

Lin Yutang *(1895–1976)* gained fame as an author and scholar. Born in Zhangzhou, China, he graduated from college in Shanghai. He earned graduate degrees from Harvard University and the University of Leipzig. After teaching English at the Beijing National University, he moved to New York and wrote many books about Chinese life and culture. One of these, *My Country and My People,* became a number-one bestseller. Some of Lin Yutang's finest stories are collected in *Famous Chinese Short Stories,* from which "The Tiger" is taken.

Magic Words
by a Netsilik Inuit

In the very earliest time,
when both people and animals lived on earth,
a person could become an animal if he wanted to
and an animal could become a human being . . .

       That was the time when words were like magic.   5
       The human mind had mysterious powers.
       A word spoken by chance
       might have strange consequences.
       It would suddenly come alive
       and what people wanted to happen could happen—   10
       all you had to do was say it.
       Nobody could explain this:
       That's the way it was.

YOU CAN ANSWER THESE QUESTIONS

Put an *x* in the box next to the correct answer.

Reading Comprehension

1. "The Tiger" takes place
   - ❏ **a.** at the present time.
   - ❏ **b.** about fifty years ago.
   - ❏ **c.** in the year 806.

2. When Chang woke up after his nap, he discovered that he
   - ❏ **a.** was in bed at the inn.
   - ❏ **b.** was no longer in China.
   - ❏ **c.** had been changed into a tiger.

3. When the tiger, Chang, knocked on the door of the temple,
   - ❏ **a.** the priest invited him in.
   - ❏ **b.** the priest refused to open the door.
   - ❏ **c.** the priest ran into the woods.

4. Which statement is true?
   - ❏ **a.** The innkeeper said that he was worried about Chang.
   - ❏ **b.** Chang spent the night in the temple.
   - ❏ **c.** Li Wen was wearing a brown suit.

5. When Chang reached the inn, he discovered that he had been gone for exactly
   - ❏ **a.** an hour.
   - ❏ **b.** eight hours.
   - ❏ **c.** twenty-four hours.

6. The governor told Li Wen's son
   - ❏ **a.** to apologize to Chang.
   - ❏ **b.** to leave and never return.
   - ❏ **c.** to appear in court.

7. At the end of the story, Li Wen's son
   - ❏ **a.** swore he would kill Chang.
   - ❏ **b.** decided not to hunt Chang anymore.
   - ❏ **c.** became one of Chang's best friends.

Vocabulary

8. The tiger crouched in the tall grass and waited for its victim. The word *crouched* means
   - ❏ **a.** bent forward.
   - ❏ **b.** fell asleep.
   - ❏ **c.** ran in circles.

9. Chang didn't like to go prowling night after night for food. The word *prowling* means
   - ❏ **a.** hunting.
   - ❏ **b.** thinking.
   - ❏ **c.** dreaming.

Idioms

10. After his meal, the tiger lay down to take a nap. The idiom *to take a nap* means to
    - ❏ **a.** watch for enemies.
    - ❏ **b.** move from place to place.
    - ❏ **c.** sleep.

How many questions did you answer correctly? Circle your score. Then fill in your score on the Score Chart on page 184.

Number Correct	1	2	3	4	5	6	7	8	9	10
Score	10	20	30	40	50	60	70	80	90	100

EXERCISES TO HELP YOU

Exercise A

Understanding the story. Answer each question by writing a complete sentence. Be sure your sentences are grammatically correct. You may look back at the story.

1. When was Chang Feng traveling in the southern part of China?

   _____

2. What did Chang do after he unpacked his luggage?

   _____

3. What did Chang realize when he woke up after his walk?

   _____

4. What happened when the tiger started to move toward the woman?

   _____

5. Where did the tiger carry Li Wen?

   _____

6. How long had Chang been away from the inn?

   _____

7. Where did Chang say he had spent the night?

   _____

8. What did Li Wen's son throw at Chang?

   _____

9. What did the governor order Li Wen's son to do?

   _____

   _____

10. What did the young man decide at the end of the story?

   _____

   _____

Exercise B

Adding vocabulary. On the left are 10 words from the story. Complete each sentence by adding the correct word.

gnawing

victim

respected

sympathize

refreshing

companions

avenge

altitude

exertion

satisfy

1. Chang felt weak from walking in a place where the

    _____ was very high.

2. Perhaps he was dizzy from the

    _____ of having walked for so long.

3. A _____ breeze made Chang feel

    less tired.

4. A terrible hunger was _____ at

    his stomach, and he knew he had to eat something

    or die.

5. He was searching for something to eat so that he

    could _____ his hunger.

6. The tiger saw Li Wen walking along the road with

    two _____.

7. The tiger knew that Li Wen would be its first

    _____.

8. The young man thought that by killing Chang he

    would _____ the death of

    his father.

9. His friends said to him, "We know how you feel,

    and we _____ with you."

10. The young man _____ his friends

    and followed their advice.

Exercise C

Part A

Combining sentences. Combine two **simple sentences** into one **compound sentence** by using a comma and the **coordinating conjunction** in parentheses (*and, but, or*). Write the compound sentence on the line. The first one has been done for you.

1. First Chang Feng unpacked his luggage. Then he took a walk in the countryside. (and)

   First Chang Feng unpacked his luggage, and then he took a walk in the countryside.

2. The tiger looked for something to eat. It was unable to find anything. (but)

   _____

   _____

   _____

3. Was he tired from walking so far? Was he affected by the color and the light? (or)

   _____

   _____

   _____

4. The tiger started to move toward the woman. She ran away from him. (but)

   _____

   _____

   _____

5. The tiger stayed in the village for a long time. Then it went back to the mountain. (and)

   _____

   _____

   _____

6. Was Li Wen traveling alone? Was he accompanied by others? (or)

_____

_____

_____

7. Chang Feng apologized to the young man. The young man refused to accept the apology. (but)

_____

_____

_____

8. The son went to the southern part of the city. Chang Feng left for the northern part. (and)

_____

_____

_____

9. The young man rushed at Chang. The other guests held him back. (but)

_____

_____

10. You must not kill Chang Feng. You will be accused of murder. (or)

_____

_____

Part B

By combining **simple sentences** into **compound sentences**, you can make your writing stronger and more interesting. Combine the following simple sentences into compound sentences by using a comma and a **coordinating conjunction** (*and, but, or*). Write the compound sentences on the lines.

11. At first Chang enjoyed being a tiger. Later he regretted it.

    _____

    _____

12. The villagers were afraid of the tiger. They locked their doors.

    _____

    _____

13. Did the tiger attack the other travelers? Did it just scare them away?

    _____

    _____

14. Chang felt sorry for Li Wen. There was nothing he could do now.

    _____

    _____

15. The son listened to his friends. He didn't bother Chang Feng anymore.

    _____

    _____

Exercise D

Finding synonyms. Read the sentence. Then select the **synonym** (the word most similar in meaning) for the word in capital letters. Circle the letter of the correct answer. Each capitalized word appears in the story.

1. Chang Feng was traveling in the southern part of China during the reign of Emperor Yuanho.

   REIGN   **a.** rule   **b.** city   **c.** leader

2. After Chang arrived at the inn, he unpacked his luggage and went outside.

   LUGGAGE   **a.** food   **b.** pockets   **c.** baggage

3. Chang strolled on and on, enjoying everything that he saw.

   STROLLED   **a.** talked   **b.** walked   **c.** dreamed

4. Chang suddenly realized that he had been transformed into a tiger.

   TRANSFORMED   **a.** attacked   **b.** worried   **c.** changed

5. He was puzzled by the strange experience.

   PUZZLED   **a.** confused   **b.** helped   **c.** learned

6. The tiger had a strong feeling that it was destined to kill Li Wen.

   DESTINED   **a.** warned   **b.** permitted   **c.** fated

7. Everyone agreed that correcting a wrong was a noble thing to do.

   NOBLE   **a.** honorable   **b.** small   **c.** interesting

8. Chang was invited to a dinner party where much wine was consumed.

   CONSUMED   **a.** dropped   **b.** swallowed   **c.** sent

9. Chang's friends persuaded him to leave the house at once.

   PERSUADED   **a.** watched   **b.** convinced   **c.** guessed

10. Because of the unusual circumstances, the son was not allowed to track down the man who had killed his father.

    CIRCUMSTANCES   **a.** conditions   **b.** threats   **c.** times

Exercise E

Understanding plot. The **plot** is the series of incidents or events in a story. How well did you understand the plot of "The Tiger"? Fill in the box next to the correct answer.

1. What happened first in the plot of the story?
   - ❑ **a.** The tiger waited in the tall grass for Li Wen.
   - ❑ **b.** Li Wen's son threw a knife at Chang Feng.
   - ❑ **c.** Chang Feng was tired and fell asleep on the grass.

2. What happened last in the plot of the story?
   - ❑ **a.** Li Wen's son returned home and spoke to his friends.
   - ❑ **b.** The tiger knocked on the door of the temple.
   - ❑ **c.** The innkeeper said that they had searched for Chang all day.

3. Which one of the following events plays the most important part in the plot of the story?
   - ❑ **a.** The priest heard a tiger knocking at the door.
   - ❑ **b.** The tiger, Chang, ate Li Wen.
   - ❑ **c.** Chang Feng decided to change his name.

4. How did Li Wen's son know that Chang was responsible for the death of his father?
   - ❑ **a.** Chang told the story at a dinner party that the son attended.
   - ❑ **b.** Some travelers told the son what had happened.
   - ❑ **c.** The innkeeper gave this information to the son.

5. How was the tiger able to recognize Li Wen?
   - ❑ **a.** The tiger had seen Li Wen before and knew who he was.
   - ❑ **b.** The tiger heard a traveler say that Li Wen was wearing green clothing.
   - ❑ **c.** Li Wen turned around when the innkeeper called his name.

6. Li Wen's son decided not to hunt Chang Feng because
   - ❑ **a.** Chang apologized to him.
   - ❑ **b.** the son was afraid of Chang.
   - ❑ **c.** the son followed the advice of his friends.

Exercise F

Vocabulary review. Write a complete sentence for each word or group of words.

1. crouched _____

   _____

2. prowling _____

   _____

3. sympathize _____

   _____

4. companions _____

   _____

5. reign _____

   _____

6. destined _____

   _____

7. circumstances _____

   _____

8. victim _____

   _____

9. exertion _____

   _____

10. took a nap _____

    _____

SHARING WITH OTHERS

This section has been designed to provide you with opportunities to share your thoughts and ideas with others, while you practice and improve your reading, writing, speaking, and listening skills.

Part A
Discuss the following questions. Share your answers with your partner or with the group.

1. "The Tiger" is a strange and unusual story. In what ways is it different from most stories you have read?

2. The author suggests that Li Wen was fated to be killed by the tiger. Find the paragraph in the story that supports this statement. Do you believe that people are unable to control their destiny, or do you believe that people, in general, can shape their fate? Explain your answer.

3. The young man was told by his friends, "Chang Feng ate your father when he was a tiger and is not responsible for his actions." Do you agree, or do you believe that Chang should have been held responsible for the death of Li Wen? Why? Explain.

4. Do you think the young man should have listened to his friends, or should he have attempted to hunt down Chang Feng? Give reasons for your answers.

5. If, for a brief period of time, you could transform yourself into an animal, what animal would you choose to be? Explain your choice.

Part B

1. On the lines below, **summarize** "The Tiger." Be sure that your summary refers to the key events in the story.

_____

_____

_____

_____

_____

_____

_____

_____

_____

_____

_____

_____

_____

_____

_____

_____

_____

_____

_____

_____

_____

2. Suppose you were a guest at the dinner party where Chang Feng told his story. On the following lines, **describe** what happened. Make your description as complete and as vivid as possible.

_____

_____

_____

_____

_____

_____

_____

_____

_____

_____

_____

_____

_____

_____

_____

_____

_____

_____

_____

_____

MAGIC WORDS

1. Read the poem again. How could people become animals and animals become people?

2. Suppose that a time actually existed when people could become animals and animals could become people. Do you think you would have liked living then? Why?

3. The poet says that words once had magic powers. Do words have "magic power" today? Think about TV, movies, books, and so forth. Explain your answer.

4. Why do you think "Magic Words" appears in a unit with "The Tiger"?

AFTER TWENTY YEARS

based on a story by O. Henry

Before You Read

Connections

Study the picture on the left. Describe what you see.

- Does this story take place in a city or in the country? Does it take place in the past or in the present? How do you know?
- What is the man doing at the left? What does he appear to be doing at the right?
- Read the title. How does the title connect to what you see in the picture? Explain.
- What will you be like in twenty years? Describe what you will be doing.

As you read, think about how the picture connects to the story.

Words to Learn

In this story, you will learn some new words. You will also learn some idioms. For example, *shows up* is an idiom that means "appears."

AFTER TWENTY YEARS

based on a story by O. Henry

Twenty years can change a man.

The time was nearly ten o'clock at night, and the streets were almost deserted. Strong gusts of wind and the threat of rain had forced most people to stay indoors. The police officer on the beat[1] moved slowly up the avenue. The guardian of the peace tried doors as he went and looked in store windows along the way.

Most of the places in the vicinity were closed. Now and then you might see lights in a luncheonette that stayed open all night, but the majority of the doors belonged to businesses that had been shut for hours.

In the middle of a certain block, the officer suddenly slowed his walk. In the dark doorway of a hardware store a man stood, with an unlighted cigar in his mouth. As the police officer walked up to him, the man spoke up quickly.

"It's all right, officer," the man said reassuringly. "I'm just waiting for a friend. It's an appointment that we made twenty years ago."

The officer looked surprised and stared at the man.

"I guess it sounds a little funny to you, doesn't it?" said the man. "Well, I can explain it. Twenty years ago there used to be a restaurant where this store is now."

"Yes," said the officer. "That was Joe Brady's Restaurant. It was here until five years ago. It was torn down then."

The man in the doorway struck a match and lit his cigar. The officer saw that the man had a pale, square face with keen eyes. There was a little scar near the man's right eyebrow. The man was

1. *beat:* As used here, the word means "a usual route or way of going."

wearing a scarf whose ends were held together by a shiny gold pin. In the center of the pin was a large, sparkling diamond.

The man said, "Exactly twenty years ago tonight I ate dinner with Jimmy Wells at Joe Brady's Restaurant here. Jimmy was my best friend and the greatest pal in the world. He and I were born in New York and grew up together. We were as close as two brothers."

The man in the doorway paused for a moment as he thought about his friend. Then he continued.

"I was eighteen and Jimmy was twenty. The next morning I was going to leave for the West to make my fortune. But you couldn't have dragged Jimmy out of New York. He thought it was the best place on earth. Well, we agreed that night that we would meet here again *exactly twenty years* from that date and time, no matter how our lives had changed, or how far we had to travel. We figured that in twenty years each of us would have his destiny worked out, whatever it might be."

"That sounds pretty interesting to me," said the officer. "But twenty years is a long time to wait before getting together. Have you heard from your friend?"

"Well, yes, for a while we corresponded. But after a year or two we stopped writing and didn't keep in touch with each other. You see, the West is a pretty big place, and I kept moving around all the time. But I know that Jimmy will meet me here if he's alive. He was always the truest, most reliable guy in the world. He'll never forget! I came a thousand miles to stand in this doorway tonight—and it will be worth it if my old friend shows up."

The man pulled out a handsome gold watch. The officer saw that the hands of the watch were made of small diamonds.

"It's three minutes before ten," the man in the doorway announced. "It was exactly ten o'clock when we left the restaurant twenty years ago."

"You did pretty well out West, didn't you?" asked the officer.

"Oh, yes! I certainly did! I hope Jimmy has done half as well. He was never as bold as me, though. I've had to compete with some of the smartest guys around. But I took some chances, made a lot of money, and came out on top. You have to be pretty sharp to do well in New York, but out West I learned how to be as sharp as a razor."

The police officer took a step or two.

"Well," he said, "I'll be going now. I hope that your friend shows up. Are you going to leave if he doesn't get here on time?"

"No, not at all," the other man said. "I'll wait at least another half an hour. If Jimmy is alive on earth, he'll be here by then. Good night, officer."

"Good night, sir," said the officer, and he moved on, trying doors as he went.

There was now a light, cold drizzle falling and the wind was beginning to blow harder. The few people in the street hurried silently and dismally along, their coat collars pulled up, their hands in their pockets. And in the doorway of the hardware store stood the man who had come a thousand miles to keep an appointment he had made twenty years go. He smoked his cigar and he waited.

He waited about twenty minutes. Then a tall man in a long overcoat, with the collar turned up to his ears, hurried across from the opposite side of the street. The tall man went straight to the man who was waiting in the doorway.

The tall man paused and then asked, "Is that you—Bob?"

"Jimmy Wells! Is that you?" exclaimed the man in the doorway. "I was sure you would come!"

The man who had just arrived threw his arms around the other man, and shook his hand. "Bob!" he said. "I was certain I would find you here if you were still alive. Well, well, well!—twenty years is a

long time. The old restaurant is gone, Bob. I wish it were still here, so we could enjoy another dinner there now."

The tall man stepped back and asked, "How has the West treated you, old pal?"

"Great! It has given me everything I wanted. You've changed quite a bit, Jimmy. You look two or three inches taller than I remembered."

"Oh, I grew a few inches after I was twenty."

"Are you doing well in New York, Jimmy?"

"Fairly well," said the tall man. "I have a job in one of the city's departments. Come on, Bob. We'll go to a place I know, and have a good long talk about old times."

The two men walked up the street, arm in arm. The man from the West, extremely pleased with his success, was talking about himself in a rather conceited way. The other man, submerged in his overcoat, listened with interest.

At the corner stood a drugstore that was bright with lights. When they came into this glare, each man turned simultaneously to look at the other man's face.

The man from the West stopped suddenly and released the other man's arm.

"You're not Jimmy Wells!" he exclaimed in distress. "Twenty years is a long time. But it's not long enough to change the shape of a man's nose."

"It sometimes changes a good man into a bad one," said the tall man.

The tall man put his arm on the other man's shoulder and said, "You've been under arrest for ten minutes, 'Silky' Bob. We heard from the Chicago police that you were heading our way, and they want to have a little talk with you there. Going quietly, are you? That's sensible. Now before we go to the station, here's a note I was asked to give to you. It's from Officer Wells."

The man from the West looked at the piece of paper the tall man gave him. His hand was steady when he began to read, but it trembled a little by the time he had finished. The note was very short.

Bob: I was at the meeting place on time. When you struck the match to light your cigar, I saw that you were the man wanted for robbery in Chicago. Somehow, I couldn't arrest you myself. So I went and got a detective to do the job.

Jimmy

Meet the Author

O. Henry (*1862-1910*) is the pen name of William Sydney Porter, one of America's most popular short-story writers. Born in Greensboro, North Carolina, O. Henry eventually moved to New York City, the setting of many of his nearly 300 stories. He wrote his first stories in an Ohio prison, where he served three years for stealing money while working as a bank teller. It is not clear if O. Henry actually stole the funds, but he fled the country and was arrested and sentenced when he returned. He subsequently took his pen name from a prison guard named Orrin Henry. O. Henry's stories are famous for the author's trademark—the surprise ending.

YOU CAN ANSWER THESE QUESTIONS

Put an *x* in the box next to the correct answer.

Reading Comprehension

1. The police officer saw a man standing in the doorway of
   - ❑ **a.** a restaurant.
   - ❑ **b.** a hardware store.
   - ❑ **c.** a drugstore.

2. How far had the man come to meet his old friend?
   - ❑ **a.** a hundred miles
   - ❑ **b.** five hundred miles
   - ❑ **c.** a thousand miles

3. How long ago had the man made the appointment?
   - ❑ **a.** ten years ago
   - ❑ **b.** twenty years ago
   - ❑ **c.** twenty-five years ago

4. How much longer was the man willing to wait for his friend?
   - ❑ **a.** a few minutes
   - ❑ **b.** at least half an hour
   - ❑ **c.** all night

5. Where was Jimmy born?
   - ❑ **a.** in New Jersey
   - ❑ **b.** in New York
   - ❑ **c.** somewhere in the West

6. Bob thought that his friend looked
   - ❑ **a.** taller.
   - ❑ **b.** shorter.
   - ❑ **c.** thinner.

Vocabulary

7. At the corner, the glare from a drugstore shone through the darkness. As used here, the word *glare* means
   - ❑ **a.** windows.
   - ❑ **b.** items for sale.
   - ❑ **c.** a bright light.

8. Each man turned simultaneously to look at the other man's face. The word *simultaneously* means
   - ❑ **a.** at the same time.
   - ❑ **b.** very slowly.
   - ❑ **c.** without interest.

Idioms

9. After a while, they stopped writing and didn't keep in touch with each other. The idiom *to keep in touch with* means
   - ❑ **a.** to communicate with.
   - ❑ **b.** to think about.
   - ❑ **c.** to need help.

10. The officer said, "I hope that your friend shows up." As used here, the idiom *shows up* means
    - ❑ **a.** remembers.
    - ❑ **b.** appears.
    - ❑ **c.** waits.

How many questions did you answer correctly? Circle your score. Then fill in your score on the Score Chart on page 184.

Number Correct	1	2	3	4	5	6	7	8	9	10
Score	10	20	30	40	50	60	70	80	90	100

Exercise A

Understanding the story. Answer each question by writing a complete sentence. Be sure your sentences are grammatically correct. You may look back at the story.

1. What did the police officer do as he walked along?

   _____

2. Why were the streets almost deserted?

   _____

3. How long ago had the man made the appointment?

   _____

4. When was Joe Brady's Restaurant torn down?

   _____

5. How old was the man when he left for the West?

   _____

6. Why didn't Jimmy want to leave New York?

   _____

   _____

7. How much longer was the man willing to wait for his friend?

   _____

   _____

8. Where did the tall man work?

   _____

9. How long had "Silky" Bob been under arrest?

   _____

10. What did Jimmy realize when Bob lit his cigar?

    _____

    _____

Exercise B

Adding vocabulary. On the left are 10 words from the story. Complete each sentence by adding the correct word.

scar	1. Since it was a cold, rainy evening, the streets were almost _____.
destiny	
compete	2. The threat of rain and strong _____ of wind kept most people indoors.
gusts	
reassuringly	
distress	3. "It's all right, officer," the man said _____.
conceited	
deserted	4. There was a little _____ near the man's right eyebrow.
razor	
sparkling	5. They believed that after twenty years each man would have his _____ worked out.

6. In the center of the gold pin was a large _____ diamond.

7. He did well, though he had to _____ with some very smart people.

8. In the West Bob learned how to be "as sharp as a _____."

9. He was extremely pleased with his success and was very _____.

10. "You're not Jimmy Wells!" he exclaimed with _____.

Exercise C

Finding synonyms. Read the sentence. Then select the **synonym** (the word most similar in meaning) for the word in capital letters. Circle the letter of the correct answer. Each capitalized word appears in the story.

1. Since it was ten o'clock at night, most of the places in the vicinity were closed.

   VICINITY   **a.** homes   **b.** city   **c.** neighborhood

2. O. Henry calls a police officer "the guardian of the peace."

   GUARDIAN   **a.** protector   **b.** fighter   **c.** hunter

3. The majority of the doors belonged to businesses that had been shut for hours.

   MAJORITY   **a.** most   **b.** some   **c.** none

4. He had come to keep an appointment they had made twenty years ago.

   APPOINTMENT   **a.** discussion   **b.** meeting   **c.** problem

5. The man from the West had a pale, square face with keen eyes.

   KEEN   **a.** sleepy   **b.** closed   **c.** sharp

6. Bob thought that Jimmy was the truest, most reliable friend in the world.

   RELIABLE   **a.** wealthy   **b.** dependable   **c.** intelligent

7. A cold drizzle was falling, and the wind began to blow harder.

   DRIZZLE   **a.** snow   **b.** rain   **c.** leaves

8. After Bob left for the West, he and Jimmy corresponded for a while.

   CORRESPONDED   **a.** wrote   **b.** argued   **c.** searched

9. He didn't think that his friend was as bold as he was.

   BOLD   **a.** fearless   **b.** calm   **c.** afraid

10. The man was submerged in a long overcoat with the collar turned up.

    SUBMERGED   **a.** warm   **b.** hidden   **c.** obvious

Exercise D

Finding antonyms. Antonyms are words with opposite meanings. For example, the words *weak* and *strong* and *up* and *down* are antonyms. Read the sentence. Then select the antonym for the word in capital letters. Circle the letter of the correct answer. Each capitalized word appears in the story. The first one has been done for you.

1. The police officer thought that the man's story was interesting.

   INTERESTING **(a.)** boring **b.** amusing **c.** fascinating

2. The man was wearing a handsome gold watch with diamonds.

   HANDSOME **a.** beautiful **b.** expensive **c.** ugly

*Did you select the **antonym**—the word that was opposite in meaning?*

3. The man from the West was pleased with his success and was talking about himself.

   SUCCESS **a.** wealth **b.** luck **c.** failure

4. In the street people hurried silently and dismally through the rain.

   DISMALLY **a.** cheerfully **b.** sadly **c.** slowly

5. Bob suddenly released the other man's arm.

   RELEASED **a.** dropped **b.** held **c.** hit

6. A man hurried across from the opposite side of the street.

   OPPOSITE **a.** same **b.** different **c.** wide

7. His hand was steady when he began reading the letter, but it trembled a little by the time he finished.

   STEADY **a.** firm **b.** shaking **c.** pointing

8. It was sensible for the man to go quietly with the detective.

   SENSIBLE **a.** smart **b.** foolish **c.** unusual

Exercise E

Critical thinking. The following questions will sharpen your **critical thinking skills.** You will have opportunities to make inferences, draw conclusions, and use hints and clues found in the story. Fill in the box next to the correct answer.

1. We may conclude that the police officer at the beginning of the story was
   - ❑ **a.** Jimmy Wells.
   - ❑ **b.** a detective.
   - ❑ **c.** Joe Brady.

2. We may infer that Jimmy Wells
   - ❑ **a.** hated "Silky" Bob.
   - ❑ **b.** was planning to change his job.
   - ❑ **c.** felt sad about having his old friend arrested.

3. Which of the following is a clue that the man in the overcoat was not Jimmy Wells?
   - ❑ **a.** The man was much heavier than Jimmy.
   - ❑ **b.** The man was shorter than Jimmy.
   - ❑ **c.** The man said that he grew a few inches after the age of twenty.

4. Which of the following is a clue that the man in the overcoat worked for the police?
   - ❑ **a.** The man said that he had a job in a city department.
   - ❑ **b.** The man looked like a detective.
   - ❑ **c.** The man was very tall.

5. We may infer that the officer asked "Silky" Bob how long he would wait for his friend because Jimmy
   - ❑ **a.** wanted to make sure that Bob would be there when the detective arrived.
   - ❑ **b.** was planning to come back in a few minutes.
   - ❑ **c.** was afraid that Bob was getting cold.

6. When Bob was out West, he "kept moving around all the time." We may infer that Bob
   - ❑ **a.** could never find a place that he liked.
   - ❑ **b.** couldn't afford to pay his rent.
   - ❑ **c.** kept moving to stay ahead of the police.

7. The name "Silky" Bob suggests that Bob was
   - ❑ **a.** not very smart.
   - ❑ **b.** very smooth and clever.
   - ❑ **c.** rough and tough.

Exercise F

Vocabulary review. Write a complete sentence for each word or group of words.

1. simultaneously _____

   _____

2. conceited _____

   _____

3. gusts _____

   _____

4. deserted _____

   _____

5. compete _____

   _____

6. distress _____

   _____

7. corresponded _____

   _____

8. submerged _____

   _____

9. dismally _____

   _____

10. kept in touch with _____

    _____

SHARING WITH OTHERS

This section has been designed to provide you with opportunities to share your thoughts and ideas with others, while you practice and improve your reading, writing, speaking, and listening skills.

Part A
Discuss the following questions. Share your answers with your partner or with the group.

1. "After Twenty Years" takes place on a very dark night. Explain why this is important to the story.

2. Bob said that he was willing to wait for his friend "at least another half an hour." Suppose Bob had told the officer that he was going to leave in five minutes. How do you think the story would have ended?

3. How did Jimmy feel about having his old friend arrested? Refer to specific details in the story to support your answer.

4. "Silky" Bob believed that he was extremely successful. Do you think that he was? Explain your answer.

5. Was Jimmy Wells right to place justice over friendship? Why? If you were Jimmy, how would you have handled the situation?

6. Borrow a collection of O. Henry's short stories from the library. Summarize one story. Be prepared to tell what happened—but don't "give away" the author's surprise ending. Some suggested stories are "The Gift of the Magi," "A Retrieved Reformation," "One Thousand Dollars," "The Cop and the Anthem," "The Last Leaf," and "The Romance of a Busy Broker."

Part B

On the following lines, write a composition comparing and contrasting Jimmy Wells and "Silky" Bob. On a separate sheet of paper, make an outline that covers their characters and careers. Work from the outline to develop your composition. Be sure to explain how Jimmy and Bob were similar and how they were different.

Comparing and Contrasting Jimmy Wells and "Silky" Bob

_____

_____

_____

_____

_____

_____

_____

_____

_____

_____

_____

_____

_____

_____

_____

_____

_____

_____

THE STOVE

based on a story by Marjorie Pickthall

Before You Read

Connections

Study the picture on the left. Describe what you see.

- At what time of year does this story take place? How do you know?
- Is the woman happy, worried, or frightened? What makes you think so?
- Will this be a funny story or a serious one? Use details from the picture to support your answer.
- Have you ever been camping? If you have, describe the experience.

As you read, think about how the picture connects to the story.

Words to Learn

In this story, you will learn some new words. You will also learn some idioms. For example, *keep your head* is an idiom that means "remain calm."

THE STOVE

based on a story by
Marjorie Pickthall

Nothing could satisfy the great iron stove.

"I'll be back with the doctor in three days at the latest. I've left you enough wood for three days and you have plenty of food." Garth looked at his sister anxiously. Suddenly he leaned forward and brushed her cheek lightly with his thick, yellow beard. "I hate to leave you," he said gently, "but I guess it's Derek's only chance."

"Of course you must go. It's Derek's only chance." Dorette faced her brother. Pale and thin, she looked weak, but she was born in the wilderness and possessed a spirit of steel.

She said quietly, "There'll be nothing for me to do, nothing—but wait."

"Only look after yourself and keep the stove going."

"I'll do it. And you—if you meet Martin Dufour—"

Rage suddenly blazed in her brother's eyes. The barrel of his rifle gleamed as he gripped it. "If I meet Martin Dufour," he said through his teeth, "it will be the end of him—or me!"

He turned without saying another word and headed down the forest trail on his way to Mandore.

Dorette watched him until he was just a dark shadow among the trees. All sound, all movement seemed to go with him. She knew that all around her, mile after mile, there was nothing but silence— the silence of the lonely and desolate forest of the North. She went into the cabin and locked the door behind her, as if the loneliness were an enemy she had to keep out.

The cabin was a pleasant place. The walls were made of red cedar, and there were four rugs on the floor and red curtains on the windows. The cabin was divided into two rooms. In the center of the

larger room stood the great iron stove. In the winter that stove kept them alive.

The roar of the stove filled the cabin like a hungry voice. Dorette swung open the heavy door and felt the heat on her face as she flung in some wood to feed the fire. That was her job now until Garth came back—feeding the stove.

She went to one of the bunks and looked down. Derek, her younger brother, lay in the bed without moving. He had been that way ever since Garth and the men had carried him in and put him there. He had been shot, and drowsed between life and death. From time to time he sipped a little soup, unaware that someone was feeding him. Dorette did not dare to touch him. There was nothing she could do for him but make sure that the cabin was warm enough to keep him alive until the doctor came, for the cold of that country kills like a sword.

At the side of the bunk she whispered, "If only you could speak to me, Derek. If only I could hear your voice."

But the only voice was the voice of the great iron stove.

She thought about the scene Garth had described to her. How Garth and the men had tracked the outlaw, Martin Dufour, to a lonely little shack in the snow. How Garth had shouted for Martin to come out of the shack. How a shot had come from nowhere, striking Derek. How the men had rushed into the shack and found it empty. Martin Dufour had escaped again! She saw it all. In her mind she saw the scene she had not witnessed. And she heard Garth's hard voice again. "But he's not going to get away this time. He'll have to get food and shelter somewhere. And if it's a thousand miles away, we'll follow and shoot him down like the wolf he is!"

She glanced around, shaken, thinking that she still heard Garth's voice filled with bitter rage. But it was only the roaring stove humming its angry song.

She busied herself, doing whatever work she could find. Twice she fed the stove from the pile of wood on the floor beside it. The fierce heat licked out at her each time, like a savage beast striking through the bars of its cage. Each time she shut the door, she felt as though she were locking up some living thing.

She glanced at the clock. Only an hour of the slow time had passed. Garth had been gone only an hour. She turned the clock toward the wall, took out a shirt she was making for Garth, and started to stitch it.

As she worked, she heard the soft thud of snow falling from trees in the forest. She could hear Derek's weak, shallow breathing. Now and then his heart seemed to pause. Then she held her breath until her brother's heart resumed its weak rhythm.

So the morning passed. In the afternoon she found a snowshoe that needed restringing. She twisted the gut and wove the net, working carefully on it.

It was dark sooner than she could have hoped. The stove filled the cabin with its glow. Glancing at the windows, she saw that they were covered with frost. It would be a cold night. She thought about Garth and then—with dread—about Martin Dufour. She dragged her cot from the other room, set it in front of the stove, and lay down. The warmth was like a hand pressing on her eyelids.

Five times during the long night, she woke up to feed the stove. The last time she awoke, the sun had risen. The frost on the window was glowing. Dorette went into the other room and combed her hair.

That day passed as the first had done, although it seemed to her that her brother looked weaker. She pleaded with him, "Take a mouthful of soup. Take it for my sake, Derek." But her voice could not reach him.

The diminished heap of logs on the floor showed that there was work for her to do. She must bring in a fresh supply from the pile of firewood behind the cabin. She ate a quick breakfast. Then, putting on her coat and hood to protect herself from the cold, she opened the door.

She stepped into a world of white, blue, and black; a world

sparkling brilliantly as though made of gems. It was fiercely cold. She shut the door behind her, ran quickly to the snow-buried woodpile behind the cabin, and gathered an armful of small logs. Then she returned to the cabin, pushed open the door, and tumbled the wood onto the floor. She worked that way all morning. As she did her spirits rose, and she began to feel better. She began to believe that Derek would not die, and remembered that Garth would return soon. She was pleased with the crashing noise the logs made as she threw them on the floor. It was a change from the one unceasing voice that filled the cabin day and night—the voice of the stove.

The second night she was restless. At first she dared not sleep, for fear that she would sleep too soundly. She could hear the wind whistling loudly. The great stove sang to a higher note. She could hardly keep up with its consuming hunger. The pine and birch logs burned to ashes in minutes. When she did sleep, she dreamed that the cold was creeping into the cabin in long fingers of frost that twisted, like snakes, under the door. One touched her on the throat and she woke up, choking.

Dawn found the sky filled with clouds, the cabin warm, the sick man still alive.

As the day went on her heart grew lighter. In four or five hours Garth should be back with the doctor from Mandore. She wound the clock and turned it so that it faced the room. She no longer dreaded seeing the passage of time.

Five hours went by and Garth had not yet arrived.

She went to the door. Closing it behind her to prevent the cold from entering the cabin for even a moment, she stared down the trail. It ran straight for less than half a mile; beyond that she could not see.

"Garth! Garth! Garth!"

Who had uttered that wild cry that echoed among the trees? She paused for a moment. Then she realized that it had come from her!

She decided she must see beyond the bend in the trail. She built up the fire, put on her coat and hood and snowshoes, took a glance at Derek, and left the cabin. She sped down the trail. She was panting when she reached the curve. Almost afraid to look, she saw the long track of footprints in the snow leading away. She saw nothing else. She did not dare to go on. She turned around and ran home.

The clock ticked off another hour—two, three, four. Garth had not returned.

Darkness, and he had not come.

Loneliness and suspense were shaking her strong, young nerves. Worst of all was the silence. The voice of the stove was at first annoying; then it became intolerable. She threw the wood in angrily. "If there was only someone to *speak* to," she said a little wildly—"just someone to give me a word!"

There was no one then—nor through the endless night.

She stayed awake all night, afraid to fall asleep, fearful that the stove that kept them alive might go out. Dawn came and Garth still was not there.

There was no wood left in the cabin. Before she did anything else, she put on her coat and went back to the woodpile.

The wood was piled high against the back of the cabin and was covered with snow. She pulled at a log and the wood came tumbling down. The hard work was a relief to her as she piled a load so heavy, she swayed under its weight. "It's something I can do for Derek," she said. "It's all I can do."

She took in enough for the day. But there was the night.

"Garth will be back by then," she muttered, staring at the stove. Just then the stove sent a screaming rush of flame up the pipe, as though it were mocking her. She felt a hatred for it as she went wearily out again to gather enough wood for the night too.

She kneeled beside the woodpile and reached in for the logs. She felt nothing but snow!

She pushed her arm into the snow up to her shoulder. Still she felt nothing but snow.

Her heart began to pound loudly. She found a long stick and prodded the pile, but still she found nothing but snow.

"How did it happen?" she asked herself over and over. Easily enough. She or Garth or Derek had been taking logs from the other side of the pile. A large drift of snow had slipped down from the roof and had filled the empty spaces in the pile. What they believed were logs was no more than a huge heap of snow.

Dorette turned slowly and went into the cabin.

She stood near Derek's bunk and stared at the wood on the floor. It was enough for the day, but what about the night?

Would Garth return before the night?

She looked around the cabin. There were things there, things that would burn. Her brown eyes grew wider. There was war in them as she leaned over and kissed Derek's cheek. He did not stir from his sleep.

"Sleep well, Derek," she whispered. "I'll take care of you."

She took Garth's heavy ax and began on the chairs.

They were heavy and clumsy things. Garth had made them himself and was proud of them. Still, they would feed the stove well. But they were hard and difficult to chop, and Dorette's hands had been scorched by the door of the stove. As she toiled, striking each blow sharply and cleanly, her eyes searched the cabin for firewood. That box could be used, that shelf, the table. The wind howled loudly outside and the day was full of sounds. Now and then she ran to the door, crying, "Garth!" But each time she saw nothing but the forest and the snow.

By early evening she had chopped up everything in the cabin. Each stroke sent pain to her shoulder from her burned and bruised hands, but she did not feel it. And still the stove roared, ever hungry. The dry wood from the cabin burned quickly, like straw. The great iron stove must be fed, and she had nothing to feed it!

She took the ax and went out.

The gray forest stood before her in snow and in shadows. There must be a hundred fallen boughs[1] within range of the cabin. She found one and dragged it from the snow into the cabin. She tore off the branches and thrust them into the stove. Blood from her hands stained the wood that she threw into the fire.

She went out again. There was a large branch hanging down from a spruce. She tore at it desperately with all her strength, but it would not move—it was frozen. She swung the ax against it again and again with all of her might until, finally, the ax handle turned in her weary hand and fell. She stood there exhausted and breathing heavily.

The bitter snow stung her face like heat—like the heat of the stove. What should she do? She knew it was important to keep her head and think. If she stayed there, the stove would go out. She turned and looked around. In the growing darkness she saw a man who stood with a rifle on his arm. He was looking at her.

"*Garth!* Oh, Garth!"

But even as the words left her lips, she knew it was not Garth.

She saw a man dressed in heavy furs, his face hidden in the hood he had drawn forward above his fur hat. He stood there silently, strangely still.

Then, suddenly, she remembered something. "The stove!" she said. "The stove!"

"What stove?"

"The stove. The stove—in our cabin. There's no more wood for the stove."

The man seemed not to understand. "The stove," she repeated, "there in the cabin. It's going out!"

Still he waited.

"There's a sick man there—my brother," she said finally. "Are you going to help me?"

---

1. *boughs:* very large branches of a tree.

She imagined, somehow, that he was laughing in the shadow of his hood. "But why should I help you?" he asked.

She had no more words. Silently she held out to him her bleeding hands.

After a long minute he stirred slowly. Without a word he placed his gun on two branches that grew above her reach. He lifted the ax from the snow, made a dozen sharp cuts, and watched the branch fall. Then, putting his foot on it, he chopped it quickly into four or five pieces. As each piece rolled free, Dorette grabbed it the way a starving woman might grab bread.

"That enough?"

She stared at him. "No, no!" she stammered. "It's not enough for the night. Cut me some more!"

She turned away and hurried toward the cabin. Halfway there he overtook her. Without a word he lifted the logs from her arms into his own. She was too tired to thank him. Without speaking she moved at his side, conscious only that help was here. She might yet save Derek.

In the cabin there was no light at all, no glow from the stove. Dorette swung open the door of the stove. She saw only a handful of gray-red ashes.

With trembling hands she grabbed a few twigs and threw them into the stove. The man who had followed her pushed her aside. She watched as he broke a few branches and coaxed them into flame. He tickled the appetite of the stove with some larger branches. Soon the fire took hold of the logs and fed upon them, hissing. He shut the door of the stove and turned to her.

She had lit a lamp and in the light stood looking at him. Her eyes were filled with gratitude.

"My brother's still living," she said, pointing to Derek in the bunk. The man's eyes did not follow the gesture as he said abruptly, "You stay here with him. I'm going to get more wood."

"You're a good man," she said. "I want to thank—"

But before she could finish speaking, he was at the door and out into the night.

He returned in half an hour, loaded down with wood. He did not speak to her, but busied himself feeding the stove. Then he picked up the ax and went out again. When he returned the second time, she was asleep.

Silent and untiring, he worked all night.

When she awoke the next morning, the man who had fed the stove all night was standing in the doorway. The door was open and there was a frosty freshness in the air. The world outside was bright with sun. A crow called in the forest. She looked at the stranger and said, "I did not mean to sleep. Why did you let me sleep while you worked?"

He said, almost roughly, "You were all tired out."

She said, "I knew you were a good man."

"Well," he answered slowly, "for one night."

His furred hood hid his face. She said, "Let me see you. Let me see your face."

"Why?"

She faltered, confused. She did not know why. "Because of what you have done—of what we owe you."

"We?"

"My brothers and I. Derek's still alive. I almost think he's sleeping better—more natural. When Garth comes home, he'll thank you too."

He had turned away from her again and was gazing down the trail. After a moment he said, "There's coffee on the back of the stove and some cornbread. You'd better eat. I've had some."

She had just reached the stove when he called, asking her to come to the door. When she joined him there, she saw again that strange look on his face that she had seen the night before.

He said quickly, "You're looking for your brother to come back?"

"Yes, yes. Any time."

"With another man?"

"With the doctor. Why?"

He raised his arm and pointed. In the glistening snow she saw two small, dark figures just rounding the curve in the trail.

Her heart was flooded with thankfulness. "Yes, yes, it's him and the doctor! Now you'll let him thank you."

Her words almost ended in a question, for she saw that he had his rifle on his arm and was putting on his snowshoes. Suddenly she felt uncomfortable. There was something in his silence, in his stillness, that was ominous and threatening.

She looked at him. In the shadow of the hood his eyes gleamed at her.

She breathed, "Who are you?"

"You'll know in a minute!"

He looked swiftly from her to the two men down the trail. They were coming on fast.

When they were so near that their faces could be seen, he quickly pushed her into the cabin. A bullet from the distance struck the snow near his feet. As a second bullet sent up a spray of dusty snow, the man raced into the forest and disappeared.

Dorette rushed to the door. She saw Garth down the trail, raising his rifle to fire again at the stranger.

"Get back!" shouted Garth. "That was Martin Dufour!"

Meet the Author

Marjorie Pickthall (*1883–1922*) was born in England, but she moved to Toronto, Canada, with her family when she was seven years old. Although Pickthall wrote poetry and novels, she is best known for her powerful short stories, many of which are set in the Canadian Northwest. "The Stove" is a good example of her writing. Pickthall, who loved the mountains and the woods, discovered that she wrote best when she was alone, surrounded by nature. She built a shack for herself under a huge pine tree. It was there that she did her writing.

Put an *x* in the box next to the correct answer.

Reading Comprehension

1. Garth told Dorette that she had enough wood for
   ❑ **a.** three days.
   ❑ **b.** a week.
   ❑ **c.** ten days.

2. Derek was unable to move because he had
   ❑ **a.** broken his leg.
   ❑ **b.** hurt his back.
   ❑ **c.** been shot.

3. Dorette's main job was to
   ❑ **a.** get Derek to a doctor.
   ❑ **b.** keep the stove burning.
   ❑ **c.** keep the cabin neat.

4. Dorette was surprised when
   ❑ **a.** she had no more food.
   ❑ **b.** there was no more wood in the woodpile.
   ❑ **c.** it was very cold outside.

5. Dorette chopped up the chairs because she
   ❑ **a.** was very angry.
   ❑ **b.** needed the wood for the stove.
   ❑ **c.** hated their appearance.

6. Who was the stranger who helped Dorette?
   ❑ **a.** one of Derek's friends
   ❑ **b.** the doctor
   ❑ **c.** Martin Dufour

Vocabulary

7. For miles around, there was nothing but the lonely and desolate forest. As used here, the word *desolate* means
   ❑ **a.** noisy.
   ❑ **b.** busy.
   ❑ **c.** empty.

8. Her brother's heart seemed to stop for a moment, but then it resumed its weak beating. The word *resumed* means
   ❑ **a.** began again.
   ❑ **b.** emptied out.
   ❑ **c.** listened to.

9. Now there were just a few logs on the floor. The large pile had diminished. The word *diminished* means
   ❑ **a.** became larger.
   ❑ **b.** became smaller.
   ❑ **c.** became better.

Idioms

10. As Dorette stood in the freezing cold, she realized that it was important to keep her head and think. When you *keep your head,* you
    ❑ **a.** remain calm.
    ❑ **b.** become frightened.
    ❑ **c.** shout for help.

How many questions did you answer correctly? Circle your score. Then fill in your score on the Score Chart on page 184.

Number Correct	1	2	3	4	5	6	7	8	9	10
Score	10	20	30	40	50	60	70	80	90	100

EXERCISES TO HELP YOU

Exercise A

Understanding the story. Answer each question by writing a complete sentence. Be sure your sentences are grammatically correct. You may look back at the story.

1. When did Garth think he would return?

   _____

   _____

2. How much food did Dorette have?

   _____

3. Why was Garth going to Mandore?

   _____

4. What had happened to Derek?

   _____

5. What was the most important thing that Dorette could do for Derek?

   _____

6. What did Dorette dream?

   _____

   _____

7. Why was Dorette afraid to fall asleep?

   _____

   _____

8. What did Dorette discover when she went to the woodpile?

   _____

9. Why couldn't Dorette see the stranger's face?

   _____

10. Where did the stranger go at the end of the story?

    _____

Exercise B

Adding vocabulary. On the left are 10 words from the story. Complete each sentence by adding the correct word.

restless

swayed

possessed

intolerable

gratitude

thud

witnessed

gems

mocking

wilderness

1. Dorette was used to hard work because she had been born in the _____ and had grown up there.

2. Although Dorette looked weak, she _____ a spirit of steel.

3. In her mind she saw the scene she had not _____.

4. The voice of the stove was at first annoying; then it became _____.

5. Everything was sparkling brilliantly as though made of _____.

6. She could hear the soft _____ of snow falling to the ground.

7. The load of logs was so heavy she _____ under its weight.

8. Dorette found it difficult to sleep, and spent a _____ night.

9. The loud screams of the stove seemed to be _____ Dorette.

10. When the stranger lighted a fire in the stove, she was filled with _____.

Exercise C

Building sentences by using connectives. Connectives are words that connect sentences smoothly and clearly. Usually, connectives appear at the beginning of a sentence, followed by a comma. Some common connectives are *therefore, however, finally, furthermore, thus, as a result,* and *moreover*. Connectives can lend style and force to your writing.

Below are 10 pairs of sentences. Begin the second sentence in each pair with the connective in parentheses. Use capital letters and commas. Write both sentences on the line. The first one has been done for you.

1. Derek was very close to death. Garth hurried to get a doctor. (therefore)

   Derek was very close to death. Therefore, Garth hurried to get a doctor.

2. The men tracked Martin Dufour to a lonely little shack. Dufour managed to escape. (however)

3. The cold in that country kills like a sword. It was important to keep the cabin warm. (therefore)

4. There was no firewood in the cabin. There was a strong possibility that the fire in the stove would die out. (as a result)

5. Dorette had difficulty falling asleep. When she slept, she had bad dreams. (moreover)

_____

_____

_____

_____

6. It was hard for Dorette to chop the branch because it was frozen. Her hands were bloody and bruised. (furthermore)

_____

_____

_____

_____

7. For a long time the stranger stared silently at Dorette. He decided to speak to her. (finally)

_____

_____

_____

_____

8. Martin Dufour was the family's enemy. Dorette didn't realize that the stranger was Dufour. (however)

_____

_____

_____

_____

9. The man threw some twigs and branches into the stove. They burst into flame. (finally)

_____

_____

_____

_____

10. Dufour realized that Garth would arrive at the cabin soon. Dufour knew that he had to leave at once. (thus)

_____

_____

_____

_____

Exercise D

Finding synonyms. Read the sentence. Then select the **synonym** (the word most similar in meaning) for the word in capital letters. Circle the letter of the correct answer. Each capitalized word appears in the story.

1. "I hate to leave you," Garth said anxiously.

   ANXIOUSLY   **a.** thoughtfully   **b.** foolishly   **c.** nervously

2. Dorette leaned over and kissed Derek's cheek, but Derek did not stir from his sleep.

   STIR   **a.** move   **b.** call   **c.** dream

3. Dorette found a long stick and prodded the pile of logs.

   PRODDED   **a.** pushed   **b.** built   **c.** leaped

4. The wood was hard and difficult to chop, but Dorette toiled on and did not stop.

   TOILED   **a.** wished   **b.** worked   **c.** sang

5. It was like a savage beast striking out through the bars of its cage.

   SAVAGE   **a.** wild   **b.** gentle   **c.** huge

6. Dorette's hands had been scorched by the door of the stove.

   SCORCHED   **a.** scratched   **b.** burned   **c.** broken

7. She pleaded with Derek, "Take a mouthful of soup."

   PLEADED   **a.** hoped   **b.** forced   **c.** begged

8. There was something in the stranger's silence that was frightening and ominous.

   OMINOUS   **a.** pleasant   **b.** surprising   **c.** threatening

9. Dorette did not answer him immediately. She was confused and she faltered.

   FALTERED   **a.** hesitated   **b.** asked   **c.** hurried

10. She moved without speaking, conscious only that help was near.

    CONSCIOUS   **a.** asleep   **b.** aware   **c.** afraid

Exercise E

Understanding characters and plot. The following questions review **characters** and **plot** in a story. Fill in the box next to the correct answer.

1. The main character in a story is the person the story is mostly about. Who is the main character in "The Stove"?
   - ❏ **a.** Dorette
   - ❏ **b.** Derek
   - ❏ **c.** Martin Dufour

2. Which description best characterizes Dorette?
   - ❏ **a.** She was lazy and hated to work.
   - ❏ **b.** She was selfish and cared only about herself.
   - ❏ **c.** She was a brave and determined person.

3. Select the statement that best characterizes Martin Dufour.
   - ❏ **a.** He was a kind man who was loved by everyone.
   - ❏ **b.** He was always friendly and helpful.
   - ❏ **c.** He was a hated outlaw who did one good deed.

4. What happened first in the plot of "The Stove"?
   - ❏ **a.** The stranger lighted a fire in the stove.
   - ❏ **b.** Garth headed down the trail toward Mandore.
   - ❏ **c.** Dorette began to chop up some of the things in the cabin.

5. What happened last in the plot of the story?
   - ❏ **a.** Garth fired a shot at Martin Dufour.
   - ❏ **b.** The stranger chopped a branch into four or five pieces.
   - ❏ **c.** Dorette stayed up all night to feed the stove.

6. Which one of the following events played the most important part in the plot of the story?
   - ❏ **a.** Dorette discovered that the woodpile was empty.
   - ❏ **b.** Dorette started to stitch a shirt she was making for Garth.
   - ❏ **c.** Dorette ran down the trail and shouted, "Garth!"

Exercise F

Vocabulary review. Write a complete sentence for each word.

1. desolate _____

_____

2. resumed _____

_____

3. gems _____

_____

4. restless _____

_____

5. gratitude _____

_____

6. intolerable _____

_____

7. toiled _____

_____

8. scorched _____

_____

9. ominous _____

_____

10. conscious _____

_____

SHARING WITH OTHERS

This section has been designed to provide you with opportunities to share your thoughts and ideas with others, while you practice and improve your reading, writing, speaking, and listening skills.

Part A

Discuss the following questions. Share your answers with your partner or with the group.

1. The stove itself may be viewed as a character in this story. Do you agree or disagree with this statement? Offer reasons to support your answer.

2. When Martin Dufour saw Dorette, he stood for a long time "silently, strangely still." What do you think that Dufour might have been thinking about? Why did he finally decide to help Dorette? Give several possible reasons.

3. Did you suspect that the stranger was Martin Dufour? If so, when did you first consider this possibility? What clues in the story suggest the stranger's identity?

4. Dorette told the stranger that he was "a good man." He responded by saying, "Well, for one night." What did each character mean? Who was right? Why?

5. Nature plays a very important role in "The Stove." Find specific examples from the story to support this statement.

6. Suppose that the stranger had not appeared. How do you think the story might have ended?

Part B

1. On the lines below, **summarize** "The Stove." Be sure that your summary refers to the key events in the story.

_____

_____

_____

_____

_____

_____

_____

_____

_____

_____

_____

_____

_____

_____

_____

_____

_____

_____

2. Refer to question 6 in Part A. On the lines below, **summarize** what happens in your new ending to the story. Try to make your conclusion as interesting as possible.

_____

_____

_____

_____

_____

_____

_____

_____

_____

_____

_____

_____

_____

_____

_____

_____

_____

_____

EARLY AUTUMN

based on a story by Langston Hughes

Before You Read

Connections

Study the picture on the left. Describe what you see.

- What clues in the picture suggest that it is autumn?
- In what way do you think the two people are related to each other?
- Does the woman on the bus look happy or sad? Why might she feel this way?
- Do you like stories about human relationships? Describe one that you have read or heard.

As you read, think about how the picture connects to the story.

Words to Learn

In this story, you will learn some new words. You will also learn some idioms. For example, *at first* is an idiom that means "immediately."

EARLY AUTUMN

by Langston Hughes

They were in love . . . a long time ago.

When Bill was very young, they had been in love. Many nights they had spent walking, talking together. Then something not very important had come between them, and they didn't speak. Impulsively, she had married a man she thought she loved. Bill went away, bitter about women.

Yesterday, walking across Washington Square, she saw him for the first time in years.

"Bill Walker," she said.

He stopped. At first he did not recognize her, to him she looked so old.

"Mary! Where did you come from?"

Unconsciously, she lifted her face as though wanting a kiss, but he held out his hand. She took it.

"I live in New York now," she said.

"Oh"—smiling politely. Then a little frown came quickly between his eyes.

"Always wondered what happened to you, Bill."

"I'm a lawyer. Nice firm, way downtown."

"Married yet?"

"Sure. Two kids."

"Oh," she said.

A great many people went past them through the park. People they didn't know. It was late afternoon. Nearly sunset. Cold.

"And your husband?" he asked her.

"We have three children. I work in the bursar's office[1] at Columbia."

"You're looking very . . ." (he wanted to say *old*) ". . . well," he said.

She understood. Under the trees in Washington Square, she found herself desperately reaching back into the past. She had been older than he then in Ohio. Now she was not young at all. Bill was still young.

"We live on Central Park West," she said. "Come and see us sometime."

"Sure," he replied. "You and your husband must have dinner with my family some night. Any night. Lucille and I'd love to have you."

The leaves fell slowly from the trees in the Square. Fell without wind. Autumn dusk. She felt a little sick.

"We'd love it," she answered.

"You ought to see my kids." He grinned.

Suddenly the lights came on up the whole length of Fifth Avenue, chains of misty brilliance in the blue air.

"There's my bus," she said.

He held out his hand, "Good-bye."

"When . . ." she wanted to say, but the bus was ready to pull off. The lights on the avenue blurred, twinkled, blurred. And she was afraid to open her mouth as she entered the bus. Afraid it would be impossible to utter a word.

1. *bursar's office:* an office, usually at a college, that receives and pays bills.

Suddenly she shrieked very loudly, "Good-bye!" But the bus door had closed.

The bus started. People came between them outside, people crossing the street, people they didn't know. Space and people. She lost sight of Bill. Then she remembered she had forgotten to give him her address—or to ask him for his—or tell him that her youngest boy was named Bill, too.

Meet the Author

Langston Hughes (*1902–1967*) was born in Joplin, Missouri, and spent his early years in Lawrence, Kansas, and Cleveland, Ohio, where he graduated from high school. It was there that his first short stories were published in the monthly literary magazine. Hughes was only nineteen years old when he wrote the powerful poem "The Negro Speaks of Rivers." Five years later, after the publication of his first book, he received a scholarship to Lincoln University. After graduating, Hughes lived in Harlem, New York City, where he became a leading figure in literature and the arts. During his career Hughes wrote short stories, poems, songs, novels, plays, articles, movie scripts, and an autobiography. In all, he published more than fifty books. His poems have been translated into almost every language, and many have been set to music. They are sad, humorous, moving, and demonstrate a deep concern for humanity.

The City
by Langston Hughes

In the morning the city
Spreads its wings
Making a song
In stone that sings.

In the evening the city   5
Goes to bed
Hanging lights
About its head.

Lonely House
by Langston Hughes

At night when everything is quiet
This old house seems to breathe a sigh.
Sometimes I hear a neighbor snoring,
Sometimes I hear a baby cry,
Sometimes I hear a staircase creaking,   5
Sometimes a distant telephone.

Then the quiet settles down again,
The house and I are all alone.

Lonely house! Lonely me!
Funny with so many neighbors   10
How lonely it can be!
Oh, lonely street! Lonely town!
Funny you can be so lonely
With all these folks around.

I guess there must be something   15
I don't comprehend. . . .
Sparrows have companions,
Even stray dogs find a friend.
The night for me is not romantic.
Unhook the stars and take them down.   20
I'm lonely in this lonely house
In this lonely town.

Declaration

by Langston Hughes

If I was a sea-lion
Swimming in the sea,
I would swim to China
And you never would see me.
    No!   5
    You never would
    See me.

If I was a rich boy
I'd buy myself a car,
Fill it up with gas   10
And drive so far, so far.
    Yes!
    I would drive
    So far.

Hard-hearted and unloving!   15
Hard-hearted and untrue!
If I was a bird I'd
Fly away from you.
    Yes, way
    Away   20
    From
    You.

Dreams
by Langston Hughes

Hold fast to dreams
For if dreams die
Life is a broken-winged bird
That cannot fly.

Hold fast to dreams   5
For when dreams go
Life is a barren field
Frozen with snow.

YOU CAN ANSWER THESE QUESTIONS

Put an *x* in the box next to the correct answer.

Reading Comprehension

1. Bill and Mary have not seen each other for
   - ❏ **a.** several days.
   - ❏ **b.** a few weeks.
   - ❏ **c.** years.

2. Where does Mary live now?
   - ❏ **a.** in Ohio
   - ❏ **b.** in Washington
   - ❏ **c.** in New York

3. What does Bill do for a living?
   - ❏ **a.** He is a lawyer.
   - ❏ **b.** He works at a college.
   - ❏ **c.** The story does not give this information.

4. Which statement is true?
   - ❏ **a.** Bill is older than Mary.
   - ❏ **b.** Mary is older than Bill.
   - ❏ **c.** Bill and Mary are about the same age.

5. Why can't Bill and Mary have dinner together one day?
   - ❏ **a.** They did not exchange addresses.
   - ❏ **b.** They are both too busy.
   - ❏ **c.** Bill never has dinner with anyone but his wife and children.

6. What is the name of one of Mary's children?
   - ❏ **a.** Lucille
   - ❏ **b.** Walker
   - ❏ **c.** Bill

7. "Early Autumn" takes place
   - ❏ **a.** in a park.
   - ❏ **b.** on a bus.
   - ❏ **c.** in an office.

Vocabulary

8. Bill says that he works in a firm, way downtown. As used here, the word *firm* means
   - ❏ **a.** very solid.
   - ❏ **b.** hard to move.
   - ❏ **c.** a law office.

9. Mary unconsciously lifts her face, as though wanting a kiss. When you do something *unconsciously,* you do it
   - ❏ **a.** very slowly and carefully.
   - ❏ **b.** without being aware that you are doing it.
   - ❏ **c.** with much sorrow and unhappiness.

Idioms

10. Bill doesn't realize that it is Mary, at first. The idiom *at first* means
    - ❏ **a.** later.
    - ❏ **b.** immediately.
    - ❏ **c.** soon.

How many questions did you answer correctly? Circle your score. Then fill in your score on the Score Chart on page 184.

Number Correct	1	2	3	4	5	6	7	8	9	10
Score	10	20	30	40	50	60	70	80	90	100

Exercise A

Understanding the story. Answer each question by writing a complete sentence. Be sure your sentences are grammatically correct. You may look back at the story.

1. Why doesn't Bill recognize Mary when she calls to him?

   _____

   _____

2. Where does Mary live now?

   _____

   _____

3. What does Bill do for a living?

   _____

   _____

4. How many children does Bill have?

   _____

   _____

5. Where does Mary work?

   _____

   _____

6. Who is older, Bill or Mary?

   _____

   _____

7. At what time of the year does the story take place?

_____

_____

8. Why is Mary afraid to open her mouth as she enters the bus?

_____

_____

9. Why can't Bill and Mary have dinner together one day?

_____

_____

_____

10. What name has Mary given to her youngest son?

_____

_____

Exercise B

Adding punctuation. The following sentences need **punctuation marks**. Add capital letters, periods, commas, question marks, exclamation points, apostrophes, and quotation marks where necessary. Write the corrected sentences on the lines.

1. mary works in the bursars office at columbia university

   _____

   _____

   _____

2. she lived in ohio but then she moved to an apartment on central park west in new york city

   _____

   _____

   _____

3. bill walker she shouts loudly at the man

   _____

   _____

   _____

4. where did you come from mary he asks

   _____

   _____

   _____

5. at first bill doesnt recognize marys face because shes gotten quite old

   _____

   _____

   _____

6. she says always wondered what happened to you bill

_____

_____

_____

7. they had spent many nights walking talking going to the movies, and eating dinner together

_____

_____

_____

8. bill a lawyer asks isnt washington square Park beautiful in autumn

_____

_____

_____

9. bills eyes meet hers as boys girls men, and women rush past them

_____

_____

_____

10. good-bye she exclaims as she boards the fifth avenue bus

_____

_____

_____

Exercise C

Finding synonyms. Read the sentence. Then select the **synonym** (the word most similar in meaning) for the word in capital letters. Circle the letter of the correct answer. Each capitalized word appears in the story.

1. It was autumn, and the leaves slowly dropped from the trees.

   AUTUMN   **a.** summer   **b.** winter   **c.** fall

2. It was difficult to see in the late afternoon dusk.

   DUSK   **a.** dark   **b.** dust   **c.** time

3. When the lights went on, they gave Fifth Avenue a certain brilliance.

   BRILLIANCE   **a.** brightness   **b.** motion   **c.** shadow

4. After Bill and Mary stopped speaking to each other, Bill went away feeling bitter about women.

   BITTER   **a.** glad   **b.** shocked   **c.** angry

5. Since the air was misty, they could not see the bus very clearly.

   MISTY   **a.** hazy   **b.** cool   **c.** dry

6. Mary impulsively married a man she thought she loved.

   IMPULSIVELY   **a.** suddenly   **b.** sadly   **c.** thoughtfully

7. The lights on the avenue twinkled like stars.

   TWINKLED   **a.** fell   **b.** started   **c.** sparkled

8. Bill grinned and said, "You ought to see my kids."

   GRINNED   **a.** shook   **b.** shouted   **c.** smiled

9. Mary was afraid to open her mouth because she feared she would be unable to utter a word.

   UTTER   **a.** spell   **b.** say   **c.** need

10. Suddenly she shrieked very loudly, "Good-bye!"

    SHRIEKED   **a.** whispered   **b.** screamed   **c.** wondered

Exercise D
Word families. Fill in the blanks by writing the correct word from each family of words. Use each word once. The first one has been done for you.

despair   despaired   desperate   desperately   desperation

1. Mary ___*despaired*___ of ever seeing Bill again.

2. She _____ wanted to discuss what had happened years ago.

3. When she realized that she might not ever see him again, she was filled with _____.

4. Mary's unusual behavior convinced her friends that she was becoming _____.

5. Calling every Bill Walker listed in the phone book was an act of

   _____.

recognize   recognized   recognizing   recognizable   recognition

6. When Mary saw Bill, she _____ him at once.

7. She succeeded in _____ Bill, although she had not seen him for years.

8. For a moment, Bill did not _____ the woman who was calling his name.

9. Langston Hughes's poems and stories have earned him worldwide

   _____.

10. Hughes has his own unique writing style. It is easily

    _____ to experts in literature.

Thinking critically. How well can you "read between the lines"? The following questions will help you think critically. Fill in the box next to the
correct answer.

1. We may infer that Mary
   ❏ **a.** no longer cared about Bill.
   ❏ **b.** never cared about Bill.
   ❏ **c.** still cared about Bill very much.

2. We may conclude that Bill
   ❏ **a.** was still in love with Mary.
   ❏ **b.** no longer cared deeply about Mary.
   ❏ **c.** wanted very much to see Mary again.

3. Mary had "impulsively married a man she thought she loved." The
   author provides this information to suggest that Mary
   ❏ **a.** hated her husband.
   ❏ **b.** loved her husband very much.
   ❏ **c.** no longer loved her husband as much as she once
       thought she did.

4. Bill's attitude toward Mary is shown by the fact that he
   ❏ **a.** did not give her a kiss, but shook her hand.
   ❏ **b.** said that she looked very well.
   ❏ **c.** told her that he was a lawyer.

5. Bill and Mary will probably
   ❏ **a.** have dinner together some time.
   ❏ **b.** never have dinner together.
   ❏ **c.** become good friends.

6. The last sentence of the story suggests that Mary
   ❏ **a.** had a bad memory.
   ❏ **b.** was trying to forget about Bill.
   ❏ **c.** had loved Bill very much.

Exercise F

Vocabulary review. Write a complete sentence for each word or group of words.

1. unconsciously _____

   _____

2. misty _____

   _____

3. dusk _____

   _____

4. impulsively _____

   _____

5. brilliance _____

   _____

6. utter _____

   _____

7. twinkled _____

   _____

8. desperately _____

   _____

9. recognition _____

   _____

10. at first _____

   _____

SHARING WITH OTHERS

This section has been designed to provide you with opportunities to share your thoughts and ideas with others, while you practice and improve your reading, writing, speaking, and listening skills.

Part A

Discuss the following questions. Share your answers with your partner or with the group.

1. What was Mary's reaction when she first saw Bill? What was Bill's reaction when he realized that the woman who was calling to him was Mary?

2. When Mary said that she lived in New York, Bill said, "'Oh'—smiling politely. Then a little frown came quickly between his eyes." What does this passage suggest?

3. When Bill asked Mary about her husband, she responded by saying, "We have three children. I work in the bursar's office at Columbia." Why do you think Mary didn't answer Bill's question directly? What does this suggest about Mary's relationship with her husband? What information in the first paragraph supports this view?

4. What invitations did Bill and Mary exchange before they parted? Do you think Mary's invitation was sincere? Was Bill's? Explain your answers.

5. Mary's chance meeting with Bill proved to be a very emotional one for her. Find specific references in the story to support this statement.

6. When Bill returns home, do you think he will tell his wife about meeting Mary? Why? If so, what do you think he will say? Will Mary tell her husband that she met Bill? Why? If so, what do you think she will say?

Part B

Relationships sometimes change a great deal with the passing of time. Think about an occasion when you met someone you had not seen for a long time—a relative, a friend, or a teacher, for example. On the lines below, write a description of the incident. Be sure your composition tells who you met, where you met, and what events led to the meeting. Were you pleased or disappointed, nervous or excited? What were some of the things you both talked about? Do you look forward to meeting that person again?

If you prefer, write about an occasion when you returned to a place you had not seen for a long time—perhaps a country, school, or house you once lived in. **Describe** the circumstances of your visit and your reactions. Provide as many **details** as you can.

When you have finished writing, think of a good title for your composition. Write it on the line provided.

_____

_____

_____

_____

_____

_____

_____

_____

_____

_____

_____

_____

_____

_____

_____

_____

_____

_____

_____

_____

_____

_____

_____

_____

Poetry

THE CITY

1. **Stanzas** are lines in a poem that go together. "The City" contains two stanzas. How many lines are there in each stanza? Which lines in each stanza rhyme?

2. Stanza 1 describes the city as it awakens. To what does the poet compare the city? Explain the meaning of "a song in stone that sings."

3. Stanza 2 describes the city as it goes to bed. What lights hang above the city's head? Think of as many as you can.

LONELY HOUSE

1. Read the song lyrics to yourself again. What mood or feeling do the words create? How many times (including the title) does the word *lonely* appear? In a sentence state what the lyrics say.

2. In what ways are "The City" and "Lonely House" similar? How are they different?

DECLARATION

1. How many stanzas are there in "Declaration"? How many lines are there in each stanza? Which lines in each stanza rhyme?

2. Why is the poem titled "Declaration"? Does the speaker in "Declaration" remind you, in any way, of Bill in "Early Autumn"? If so, explain how.

DREAMS

1. How many stanzas are there in "Dreams"? How many lines are there in each stanza? Which lines in each stanza rhyme?

2. A **metaphor** compares two things without using the words *like* or *as*. "Life is a broken-winged bird" is a metaphor. Find another metaphor in the poem.

3. A **simile** compares two things by using the words *like* or *as*. Change the metaphors in the poem to similes.

4. Langston Hughes has written hundreds of poems. "Dreams" is one of his most popular and best loved. Why do you think this poem is so popular?

AN OCCURRENCE AT OWL CREEK BRIDGE

based on a story by Ambrose Bierce

Before You Read

Connections

Study the picture on the left. Describe what you see.

- Who do you think the man is between the two soldiers?
- What do you think is going to happen to the man? Point out details in the picture to support your answer.
- Notice the man swimming in the water. Who do you think he is?
- Do you prefer happy stories or sad stories? Why?

As you read, think about how the picture connects to the story.

Words to Learn

In this story, you will learn some new words. You will also learn some idioms. For example, *to have one's heart set on* is an idiom that means "to desire greatly."

AN OCCURRENCE AT OWL CREEK BRIDGE

based on a story
by Ambrose Bierce

He was waiting to die.

Part 1

A man stood on a bridge in northern Alabama, looking down into the swift water twenty feet below. The man's hands were behind his back, his wrists tied together with a cord. There was a rope around his neck. It was attached to a wooden beam above his head.

The man was standing on some boards that served as a temporary platform. Also on the platform were the men who were going to hang him—soldiers of the Union Army.[1] A sergeant was directing two of the soldiers. A short distance away from them was a captain who stood silently, his arms folded. At each end of the bridge was a guard holding a rifle. The guard's job was to prevent anyone from coming onto the bridge.

The man who was about to be hanged was about thirty-five years of age. He was not wearing a uniform and, judging from his clothes, was quite wealthy. He was a handsome man whose long dark hair was combed straight back. It fell behind his ears to the collar of his well-fitting coat. He had a moustache and a pointed beard, and his large dark-gray eyes had a kindly expression. Clearly, this was no common killer.

The preparations were now complete. The two soldiers looked at the sergeant. The sergeant turned to the captain, saluted, and waited for the signal—the signal that would send the condemned man to his death.

1. *Union Army:* The army of the North during the Civil War (1861–1865). The Union Army fought against the Confederate Army—the army of the South.

The man glanced down at the swirling water of the stream below. A piece of drifting wood caught his attention. His eyes followed it as it bobbed up and down in the current. How slowly it seemed to move! What a sluggish stream!

The man closed his eyes and fixed his last thoughts on his wife and children. The water, sparkling brightly in the sun, had bothered him. And now, something new distracted him. It was a sound that he could neither understand nor ignore—a sharp, loud banging, like a hammer pounding. It had the same ringing sound. He wondered what it was and whether it was far away or near, for it seemed to be both. The sounds grew louder and stronger. They stabbed his ears like the jabs of a knife. He was afraid that he would scream. What he heard was the ticking of his watch.

He opened his eyes and again saw the water below him. "If I could free my hands," he thought, "I could pull off this noose and jump into the stream. By diving under the water, I could evade the bullets. I could swim swiftly to the shore, run into the woods, and get away to my home. My home, thank goodness, is still outside their lines. My wife and children are still far away from the enemy."

These thoughts flashed into the doomed man's brain. And as they did, the captain nodded to the sergeant and gave the signal.

Part 2

Peyton Farquhar was a wealthy farmer. He came from an old and highly respected Alabama family. Farquhar was a Southerner who believed very strongly in the cause of the South. Certain things had happened that prevented him from joining the army and taking part in the fight against the North. Farquhar hated this, for he longed to be a soldier. Meanwhile, he did what he could and waited for an opportunity to serve the South. He was sure that the opportunity would come. Then he would do whatever he was asked, would be willing to face any danger.

One evening Farquhar and his wife were sitting on a bench near the entrance to his land. Just then a soldier dressed in gray rode up to the gate and asked for a drink of water. Mrs. Farquhar was happy to serve the soldier, for his gray uniform revealed that he was a soldier from the South. While she was getting the water, Farquhar approached the dusty horseman and inquired eagerly for news from the front.

The man shook his head and said, "Soldiers from the North are getting ready to advance. They have reached the Owl Creek bridge and are preparing to send soldiers and supplies over it. Their commander has issued an order, which has been posted everywhere. I saw the order. It warns everyone to stay away from the bridge. Anyone caught interfering with the bridge will be hanged."

"How far is it to the Owl Creek bridge?" asked Farquhar.

"About thirty miles."

"Are there many soldiers from the North on this side of the bridge?"

"There is just a small squad half a mile away. And there is one guard with a rifle at this end of the bridge."

"Suppose a man could get around the squad? Suppose he was able to overpower the guard," said Farquhar, smiling. "What could he do then? What could he accomplish?"

The soldier thought for a moment. "He could do much damage," he said. "He could destroy the bridge and prevent the North from advancing. I was there a month ago. I noticed that last winter's flood had thrown a great deal of driftwood against the wooden pier of the bridge. It is now very dry and would burn very quickly."

Farquhar smiled again, and at that moment his wife returned with the water, which the soldier drank. He thanked her politely, bowed to them both, then rode away. An hour later, when it was dark, he headed back in the direction from which he had come. The man was a spy—a spy *for the North!*

Part 3

As Peyton Farquhar fell straight down from the bridge, he lost consciousness and was as one already dead. He was awakened from this state—ages later, it seemed to him—by a sharp pain in his throat.

He also felt as though he were choking. Pain seemed to shoot downward from his neck to every part of his body. He could not think, could only feel, and what he felt was torment.

And then, suddenly, he became aware that he was falling. All at once, the light around him flashed upward, and there was a loud splash. There was a roaring in his ears and everything was cold and dark.

Suddenly he could think again. He knew that the rope had broken and that he had fallen into the stream. The noose around his neck was choking him, but it kept the water from reaching his lungs. To die of hanging at the bottom of a river!—The idea seemed crazy, absurd to him. He opened his eyes and saw above him a gleam of light—but how distant it was, how far away. He was still sinking, for the light was getting fainter and fainter, until it was merely a glimmer. Then the light began to grow brighter and he knew that he was rising to the surface of the water. He regretted that because he knew that the soldiers would see him. "To be hanged and drowned," he thought, "that is not so bad. But I do not wish also to be shot. No, I will not be shot. That is not fair."

A sharp pain in his wrists told him that he was trying to free his hands. He was not even aware that he was trying to do that. It was as though someone else were involved in the struggle. Still, he tried with all his strength to get free. And then the cord fell away, his arms parted, and he floated upward. As the light grew brighter, he could see his hands. They tore at the noose around his neck. They ripped off the rope.

His neck ached horribly and his brain was on fire. His heart felt as though it were going to explode. But his hands pounded fiercely at the water, beating it downward, forcing him up to the surface. He felt his head emerge; it was now out of the water. His eyes were blinded by the sunlight. He took a huge breath and filled his lungs with air.

He was now in control of himself. He felt the water rippling against his face, heard the sound as the water splashed against him. He looked at the forest on the bank of the river. He saw the trees, saw them clearly, saw the leaves with the insects on them. He saw flies and gray spiders spinning their webs from twig to twig. He saw rainbow-colored dewdrops glistening on the blades of grass. A fish slid along beneath his eyes and he heard the rush of its body moving through the water.

He had come to the surface facing down the stream. He turned his head and saw the bridge. He saw the soldiers on the bridge, the captain, and the sergeant. He saw their dark shadows against the blue sky. They shouted and pointed at him. The captain had drawn his pistol, but he did not fire.

Suddenly he heard a sharp cracking sound and something struck the water a few inches away from his face. He heard a second shot and saw one of the guards, his rifle raised, a thin cloud of blue smoke rising from the mouth of the gun. The man in the water saw the eye of the guard gazing at him through the sights of the rifle. He saw that it was a gray eye, and he remembered having read that gray eyes were the sharpest, that all famous sharpshooters had them. Still, this one had missed.

A current had caught Farquhar and turned him halfway around. He was now looking toward the forest. Suddenly the sound of a high, clear voice rang out behind him. It traveled loudly and distinctly across the water.

Although he was no soldier, Farquhar knew the meaning of *that* command. His body turned cold as he heard those cruel words:

"Attention company! . . . Ready! . . . Aim! . . . *Fire!*"

Part 4

Farquhar dived—dived as deeply as he could. The water roared like thunder in his ears, but still he heard the dull sound of shots. He rose again to the surface, and as he did, shining bits of metal hit him on the face and hands.

Gasping for breath, he looked around and saw that he had drifted further down the stream, nearer to safety. The soldiers had almost finished reloading their rifles. They fired again, but did not hit him.

The hunted man saw all this over his shoulder. He was now

swimming strongly, vigorously, with the current. Suddenly he felt himself whirling around and around, spinning like a top. The water, the forest, the faraway bridge, the men—all of them flew by his eyes in a blur. He was being whirled with such speed, he felt dizzy and sick. Then, suddenly, he was flung up onto the shore far away from his enemies. He was safe, but could hardly believe it. He dug his fingers into the sand and threw handfuls of it all over himself. He shouted with joy! He wept with delight!

He looked around at the trees near him on the shore. They seemed to him like giant garden plants. A strange, beautiful light shone through their branches; the breeze rustling through the leaves was like music to his ears. He would have liked to remain in that enchanted spot.

Shots in the branches high above his head caused him to change his mind at once. He quickly jumped to his feet, rushed further up the shore, and plunged into the forest.

All that day he traveled. The forest seemed interminable; it went on and on forever. Nowhere could he find a break in the woods, not even a path. He had not known that he lived in so wild a region. There was something strange in this discovery.

By nightfall he was aching, fatigued, and very hungry, but he had his heart set on seeing his wife and children, and that urged him on. At last he found a road that led in what he knew was the right direction. It was as wide and straight as a city street, yet there was no one on it. There were no houses anywhere. He did not even hear the barking of a dog.

His neck was in pain, and when he lifted his hand to it, he found that it was very sore. He knew that there must be a black circle where the rope had been tied around it. His eyes felt so swollen he could no longer close them. His tongue was hot and dry with thirst. He opened his mouth to let in some air. How soft the grass was on the path. He could no longer feel the road beneath his feet! Probably, even though he was suffering, he had fallen asleep while walking.

Now he sees another scene. He stands at the gate of his own house. Everything is just as he left it, bright and beautiful in the morning sunlight. He must have traveled the entire night. He pushes open the gate and walks up the wide white walk. He sees a flutter of female clothing and his wife, looking fresh and cool and sweet, comes down from the porch to meet him. At the bottom of the steps she stands waiting. Her face is smiling and filled with joy. Ah, how beautiful she is! He rushes forward with extended arms. As he is about to hug her, he feels a stunning blow on the back of his neck. A blinding white light blazes all around him. There is a loud, crashing sound—then all is darkness and silence!

Peyton Farquhar was dead. His body, with a broken neck, swung gently from side to side beneath the timbers of the Owl Creek bridge.

Meet the Author

Ambrose Bierce (*1842–1914*) lived a life as strange as many of the short stories he wrote. Bierce was born in a log cabin in Chester, Ohio, the tenth of thirteen children, all of whom had first names beginning with the letter *A*. Bierce did not get along with his family; and at the age of fifteen, he left home when he found a full-time job. After serving in the Civil War, which provided the background for many of his finest stories, Bierce moved to California, where he worked on newspapers and wrote short stories. He achieved fame— and became known as "Bitter Bierce"—for writing horrifying tales that had shocking and terrifying endings. In December 1913 Bierce left San Francisco for Mexico, where he disappeared. Nobody has ever discovered how or when he died.

You can answer these questions

Put an *x* in the box next to the correct answer.

Reading Comprehension

1. How old was Peyton Farquhar?
   - ❏ **a.** about twenty years old
   - ❏ **b.** about thirty-five years old
   - ❏ **c.** about fifty years old

2. The ringing sound that Farquhar heard was a
   - ❏ **a.** hammer pounding.
   - ❏ **b.** rifle firing.
   - ❏ **c.** watch ticking.

3. Which statement is not true?
   - ❏ **a.** Farquhar was a wealthy farmer.
   - ❏ **b.** Farquhar came from an Alabama family.
   - ❏ **c.** Farquhar believed in the cause of the North.

4. During the course of the story, Farquhar imagined that
   - ❏ **a.** the rope broke.
   - ❏ **b.** his friends saved his life.
   - ❏ **c.** the soldiers decided to let him go.

5. At the end of the story, Farquhar
   - ❏ **a.** was hanged and died.
   - ❏ **b.** escaped and returned home.
   - ❏ **c.** shot one of the soldiers.

Vocabulary

6. By diving under the water, he hoped to evade the bullets. The word *evade* means
   - ❏ **a.** feel.
   - ❏ **b.** see clearly.
   - ❏ **c.** get away from.

7. His gray uniform revealed that he was a soldier from the South. The word *revealed* means
   - ❏ **a.** showed.
   - ❏ **b.** helped.
   - ❏ **c.** honored.

8. He was choking and his body was filled with torment. The word *torment* means
   - ❏ **a.** interest.
   - ❏ **b.** pain.
   - ❏ **c.** information.

9. His head began to emerge; soon it was out of the water. The word *emerge* means
   - ❏ **a.** bleed.
   - ❏ **b.** hurt.
   - ❏ **c.** come up.

Idioms

10. Farquhar had his heart set on seeing his family. The idiom *to have one's heart set on* means
   - ❏ **a.** to feel weak.
   - ❏ **b.** to desire greatly.
   - ❏ **c.** to worry about.

How many questions did you answer correctly? Circle your score. Then fill in your score on the Score Chart on page 184.

Number Correct	1	2	3	4	5	6	7	8	9	10
Score	10	20	30	40	50	60	70	80	90	100

Exercise A

Understanding the story. Answer each question by writing a complete sentence. Be sure your sentences are grammatically correct. You may look back at the story.

1. Where was the bridge located?

   _____

2. What was the job of the guards who stood at each end of the bridge?

   _____

   _____

3. How old was the man who was about to be hanged?

   _____

4. What was the ringing sound that Farquhar heard?

   _____

5. According to the order, what would happen to anyone caught interfering with the bridge?

   _____

   _____

6. How far was it from Farquhar's land to the Owl Creek bridge?

   _____

   _____

7. How would destroying the bridge have helped the South?

   _____

8. Who was the soldier in gray who rode up to Farquhar's gate?

   _____

9. What did Farquhar think had happened to the rope?

   _____

10. Whom did Farquhar think he saw just before he died?

    _____

Exercise B

Adding vocabulary. On the left are 10 words from the story. Complete each sentence by adding the correct word.

condemned

sluggish

absurd

distracted

interfering

temporary

jabs

interminable

glimmer

rustling

1. The stream moved slowly; it was a

   _____ stream.

2. His thoughts were interrupted by loud banging

   sounds that _____ him.

3. The sounds stabbed his ears like the

   _____ of a knife.

4. The boards would soon be removed; they formed

   only a _____ platform.

5. The order was intended to discourage anyone from

   _____ with the bridge.

6. To die of hanging at the bottom of a river seemed

   _____ to him.

7. The light got fainter and fainter until it was only a

   _____.

8. The forest seemed _____; it went

   on and on forever.

9. The breeze _____ through the

   leaves was like music to his ears.

10. A signal from the captain would send the

    _____ man to his death.

Exercise C

Part A

Building sentences. Combine two **simple sentences** into one **complex sentence** by using the **subordinating conjunction** in parentheses. Put the conjunction in the middle of the sentence. Then write the complex sentence on the line. The first one has been done for you.

Common Subordinating Conjunctions

after	since
although	so that
because	until
if	while

1. Farquhar was going to be hanged. He had disobeyed the commander's order. (because)

   Farquhar was going to be hanged because he had disobeyed the commander's order.

2. The man's wrists were tied together with a cord. He was helpless. (so that)

3. Farquhar wanted to join the army. He longed to be a soldier. (, since)

4. His wife gave the soldier some water. Farquhar spoke to the soldier. (while)

5. Farquhar hoped to escape. That was impossible. (, although)

6. The soldiers couldn't see Farquhar. He ran into the forest. (after)

_____

_____

7. Farquhar swam with the current. He was thrown up onto the shore. (until)

_____

_____

8. He would be able to get home safely. He could escape into the woods. (if)

_____

_____

Part B

Combine the **simple sentences** into **complex sentences** by using the **subordinating conjunctions** below. Put the correct conjunction in the middle of each sentence. Then write the sentence on the line. Use each conjunction once.

> after   so that   until   while

9. He thought about his wife. He stood on the bridge.

_____

_____

10. Farquhar shouted with joy. He safely reached the shore.

_____

_____

11. He hid in the forest. The soldiers could not see him.

_____

_____

12. Farquhar didn't stop running. He came to the gate of his house.

_____

_____

Exercise D

Finding synonyms. Read the sentence. Then select the **synonym** (the word most similar in meaning) for the word in capital letters. Circle the letter of the correct answer. Each capitalized word appears in the story.

1. Farquhar felt himself whirling around and around like a toy.

   WHIRLING   **a.** turning   **b.** jumping   **c.** dancing

2. At the end of the day he was aching, fatigued, and very hungry.

   FATIGUED   **a.** bored   **b.** tired   **c.** amused

3. Farquhar saw a gray eye gazing at him.

   GAZING   **a.** looking   **b.** closing   **c.** remembering

4. The sound traveled loudly and distinctly across the water.

   DISTINCTLY   **a.** calmly   **b.** quickly   **c.** clearly

5. Farquhar approached the man and inquired whether he had any news.

   INQUIRED   **a.** paid   **b.** read   **c.** asked

6. What could a man accomplish if he were able to overpower the guard?

   ACCOMPLISH   **a.** do   **b.** want   **c.** steal

7. A blinding white light blazes all around him.

   BLAZES   **a.** opens   **b.** glows   **c.** ends

8. Farquhar jumped up quickly and plunged into the forest.

   PLUNGED   **a.** fell   **b.** searched   **c.** rushed

9. He looked down at the swirling waters of the stream.

   SWIRLING   **a.** empty   **b.** twisting   **c.** warm

10. Farquhar saw giant plants in that strange and wonderful enchanted place.

    ENCHANTED   **a.** dull   **b.** foolish   **c.** magical

Exercise E

Thinking critically. How well did you understand "An Occurrence at Owl Creek Bridge"? This story, more than most, requires the reader to think critically. Fill in the box next to the correct answer.

1. We may infer that Peyton Farquhar was hanged because he
   - ❏ **a.** was a spy for the South.
   - ❏ **b.** refused to help the North.
   - ❏ **c.** was caught attempting to destroy the Owl Creek bridge.

2. Where does most of the action of the story take place?
   - ❏ **a.** in Peyton Farquhar's mind
   - ❏ **b.** on a battlefield
   - ❏ **c.** in a forest

3. The main action of the story takes place over
   - ❏ **a.** a few seconds.
   - ❏ **b.** several weeks.
   - ❏ **c.** a few months.

4. We may infer that Peyton Farquhar died thinking about
   - ❏ **a.** his children.
   - ❏ **b.** his wife.
   - ❏ **c.** the spy who told him about the bridge.

5. Immediately before Farquhar died, he
   - ❏ **a.** almost escaped.
   - ❏ **b.** shouted at the soldiers.
   - ❏ **c.** began to imagine.

6. "An Occurrence at Owl Creek Bridge" is different from most stories in that it
   - ❏ **a.** has no main character.
   - ❏ **b.** is very short.
   - ❏ **c.** moves back and forth in time.

Exercise F

Vocabulary review. Write a complete sentence for each word or group of words.

1. evade _____

   _____

2. revealed _____

   _____

3. emerge _____

   _____

4. sluggish _____

   _____

5. absurd _____

   _____

6. interfering _____

   _____

7. temporary _____

   _____

8. accomplish _____

   _____

9. interminable _____

   _____

10. had his (or her) heart set on _____

    _____

    _____

Sharing with Others

This section has been designed to provide you with opportunities to share your thoughts and ideas with others, while you practice and improve your reading, writing, speaking, and listening skills.

Part A
Discuss the following questions. Share your answers with your partner or with the group.

1. A **flashback** interrupts a story to show an event or events that happened earlier. How many parts are there in "An Occurrence at Owl Creek Bridge"? Which part is a flashback? Explain how a flashback can add interest and power to a story.

2. Read the last sentence in Part 1. Then read the last sentence of the story again. How much time takes place between these two sentences? Where does most of the action of the story take place?

3. At some point while reading the story, did you think that Peyton Farquhar had escaped, or were you aware all along that he had never really left the bridge? Explain.

4. Were you disappointed that Farquhar did not escape? Why? If he had escaped, do you think this would have weakened the story, or would it have made it stronger? Explain.

5. Do you think that Farquhar's dream made it easier for him to face death? Why? Explain how the description of Farquhar's wife immediately before he died made his death sadder and more shocking.

6. Research the life of the author, Ambrose Bierce. Write a brief summary in outline form. Be prepared to tell three facts not stated in "Meet the Author."

Part B

1. On the lines below, **describe** how Peyton Farquhar attempted to burn down the Owl Creek bridge and was caught. Use your imagination to make the description of the incident as vivid and exciting as possible.

_____

_____

_____

_____

_____

_____

_____

_____

_____

_____

_____

_____

_____

_____

_____

_____

_____

_____

_____

_____

2. Suppose there were a Part 5 of "An Occurrence at Owl Creek Bridge." What do you think would happen? Think about how the story might continue. Then write the opening paragraph of that section.

_____

_____

_____

_____

_____

_____

_____

_____

_____

_____

_____

_____

_____

_____

_____

_____

_____

_____

_____

_____

_____

_____

_____

_____

TA-NA-E-KA

Based on a story by Mary Whitebird

Before You Read

Connections

Study the picture on the left. Describe what you see.

- Where does this story take place? What clues help you guess?
- Which person in the picture is the main character of the story?
- Does the girl appear to be enjoying herself outdoors? How can you tell?
- Do the hamburger and milkshake seem out of place to you? Why or why not?
- Do you have any family traditions? Describe one.

As you read, think about how the picture connects to the story.

Words to Learn

In this story, you will learn some new words. You will also learn an idiom. For example, *take someone's side* is an idiom that means "agree with someone."

TA-NA-E-KA

by Mary Whitebird

Only the strongest and smartest could survive.

My birthday was approaching and I had awful nightmares about it. I was reaching the age at which all Kaw Indians had to participate in Ta-Na-E-Ka. Well, perhaps not all Kaws. Some of the younger families on the reservation were beginning to give up the old customs. But my grandfather, Amos Deer Leg, was devoted to tradition. He still wore handmade beaded moccasins instead of shoes, and kept his iron gray hair in tight braids. He could speak English, but he spoke it only with white men. With his family he used a Sioux dialect.

Grandfather was one of the last living Indians (he died when he was 81) who actually fought against the U.S. Cavalry. At the time, my grandfather was only eleven years old.

Eleven was a magic word among the Kaws. It was the time of Ta-Na-E-Ka, the "flowering of adulthood." It was the age, my grandfather informed us hundreds of times, "when a boy could prove himself to be a warrior and a girl took the first steps to womanhood."

"I don't want to be a warrior," my cousin, Roger Deer Leg, confided to me. "I'm going to become an accountant."

"None of the other tribes make girls go through the endurance ritual,"[1] I complained to my mother.

"It won't be as bad as you think, Mary," my mother said, ignoring my protests. "Once you've gone through it, you'll certainly never forget it. You'll be proud."

1. *endurance ritual:* a test to see how strong one is.

I even complained to my teacher, Mrs. Richardson. I thought that, as a white woman, she would take my side.

She didn't. "All of us have customs of one kind or another," Mrs. Richardson said. "And look at it this way: How many girls have the opportunity to compete on equal terms with boys? Don't look down on your heritage."

Heritage, indeed! I had no intention of living on a reservation for the rest of my life!

But I was impressed with the way the Kaw treated women. No other Indian tribe treated women more "equally" than the Kaw. Unlike most of the tribes of the Sioux Nation, the Kaw allowed men and women to eat together. And even hundreds of years ago, a Kaw woman had the right to refuse to marry the man her father had chosen to be her husband.

The wisest women (generally the oldest) often sat in tribal councils. And most Kaw legends were about "Good Woman," a kind of superwoman who led Kaw warriors into battle after battle from which they always seemed to emerge victorious.

Girls as well as boys were required to go through Ta-Na-E-Ka. The ceremony varied from tribe to tribe, but since the Indians' life on the plains was one of survival, Ta-Na-E-Ka was a test of survival.

"Endurance is the greatest virtue of the Indian," my grandfather explained. "To survive, we must endure. When I was a boy," he went on, "Ta-Na-E-Ka was harder than it is now. We were painted white with the juice of a sacred herb and were sent naked into the wilderness without even a knife. We couldn't return until the white had worn off. It wouldn't wash off! It took almost eighteen days. During that time we had to stay alive—trapping food, eating insects and roots and berries, and watching out for enemies. And we did have enemies—the white soldiers and the Omaha[2] warriors, who were always trying to capture Kaw boys and girls undergoing their endurance test. It was an exciting time."

"What happened if you couldn't make it?" Roger asked. He was born only three days after I was, and we were being trained for Ta-Na-E-Ka together. I was happy to know he was frightened too.

"Many didn't return," Grandfather said. "Only the strongest and smartest made it. Mothers were not allowed to weep over those who didn't return. If a Kaw couldn't survive, he or she wasn't worth weeping over. It was our way."

"What a lot of hooey,"[3] Roger whispered. "I'd give anything to get out of it."

"I don't think we have any choice," I replied.

Roger gave my arm a little squeeze. "Well, it's only five days."

Five days! Maybe it was better than being painted white and sent out naked for eighteen days. But not much better.

We were to be sent, barefoot and in bathing suits, into the woods. For five days we'd have to live off the land, keeping warm as best we could, getting food where we could. It was May, but the days were still chilly and the nights were fiercely cold.

Grandfather was in charge of the month's training for Ta-Na-E-Ka. One day he caught a grasshopper and demonstrated how to pull its legs and wings off in one flick of the fingers and how to swallow it.

I felt sick, and Roger turned green. I told Roger teasingly, "You'd make a terrible warrior." Roger just made a face.

I knew one thing. I wasn't going to swallow a grasshopper no matter how hungry I got. And then I had an idea. Why hadn't I thought of it before? I would have saved nights of bad dreams about eating grasshoppers.

I headed straight for my teacher's house. "Mrs. Richardson," I said, "would you lend me five dollars?"

"Five dollars!" she exclaimed. "What for?"

"You remember the ceremony I talked about?"

2. *Omaha:* This refers to a Native American tribe that lived in northeastern Nebraska.
3. *hooey:* nonsense.

"Ta-Na-E-Ka. Of course. Your parents have written me and asked me to excuse you from school so you can participate in it."

"Well, I need some things for the ceremony," I replied, in a half-truth. "I don't want to ask my parents for the money."

"It's not a crime to borrow money, Mary. But how can you pay it back?"

"I'll baby-sit for you."

"That's fair," she said, going to her purse and handing me a crisp, new, five-dollar bill. I'd never had that much money at once.

"I'm happy to know the money's going to be put to a good use," Mrs. Richardson said.

A few days later, Ta-Na-E-Ka began. It started with a long speech from my grandfather about how we had reached the age of decision, how we now had to prove that we could take care of ourselves and survive. All the friends and relatives who had gathered at our house for dinner made jokes about their own Ta-Na-E-Ka experiences. They all advised us to eat well now, since for the next five days we'd be dining on crickets. Neither Roger nor I was very hungry. "I'll probably laugh about this when I'm an accountant," Roger said, trembling.

"Are you trembling?" I asked.

"What do you think?"

"I'm happy to know boys tremble too," I said.

At six the next morning we kissed our parents and went off to the woods. "Which side do you want?" Roger asked. According to the rules, Roger and I would each have our own "territories" in separate areas of the woods, and we weren't allowed to communicate with each other.

"I'll go toward the river, if it's okay with you," I said.

"Sure," Roger answered. "What difference does it make?"

To me, it made a lot of difference. There was a marina[4] a few miles up the river and there were some boats there. At least, I hoped so. I figured that I'd rather sleep in a boat than under a pile of leaves.

As we came to a fork in the trail, Roger shook my hand. "Good luck, Mary."

"N'ko-n'ta," I said. It was the Kaw word for *courage*.

The sun was shining and it was warm, but my bare feet began to hurt immediately. I spied one of the berry bushes Grandfather had told us about. "You're lucky," he had said. "The berries are ripe in the spring, and they are delicious and nourishing." They were orange and fat and I popped one into my mouth.

Argh! I spat it out. It was awful and bitter, and even grasshoppers probably tasted better, although I never intended to find out.

I sat down to rest my feet. A rabbit hopped out from under the berry bush. He poked the berry with his nose, then ate it. He picked another one and ate that too. He liked them. He looked at me while he twitched his nose. I watched a redheaded woodpecker tapping at an elm tree, and I caught a glimpse of a raccoon scampering through some twigs. All of a sudden I realized I was no longer frightened. Ta-Na-E-Ka might be more fun than I'd anticipated. I got up and headed toward the marina.

"Not one boat," I said to myself dejectedly. But the restaurant on the shore, "Ernie's Riverside," was open. I walked in, feeling silly in my bathing suit. The man at the counter was big and tough-looking. He wore a sweatshirt with the words "Fort Sheridan" on it. He asked me what I wanted.

"A hamburger and a milk shake," I said, holding the five-dollar bill in my hand so he'd know I had money.

"That's a pretty heavy breakfast," he murmured.

"That's what I always have for breakfast," I lied.

"Forty-five cents," he said, bringing me the food. (Back then, hamburgers were twenty-five cents and milk shakes were twenty cents.) "Delicious," I thought. "Better than grasshoppers—and Grandfather never once mentioned that I couldn't eat hamburgers!"

4. *marina:* a dock for boats.

While I was eating, I had a terrific idea. Why not sleep in the restaurant? I went to the ladies' room and made sure that the window was unlocked. Then I went back outside and played along the riverbank. I watched the water birds and tried to identify each one. I planned to look for a beaver dam the next day.

The restaurant closed at sunset, and I watched the man drive away. Then I climbed in the unlocked window. There was a night light on, so I didn't turn on any lights. But there was a radio on the counter. I turned it on to a music program. It was warm in the restaurant, and I was hungry. I helped myself to a glass of milk and a piece of pie, intending to keep a list of what I'd eaten so I could leave money. I also planned to get up early, sneak out through the window, and head for the woods before the man returned. I turned off the radio, wrapped myself in the man's apron, and in spite of the hardness of the floor, fell asleep.

"What are you doing here, kid?"

It was the man's voice.

It was morning. I'd overslept. I was scared.

"Hold it, kid. I just want to know what you're doing here. You lost? You must be from the reservation. Your folks must be worried sick about you. Do they have a phone?"

"Yes, yes," I answered. "But don't call them."

I was shivering. The man, who told me his name was Ernie, made me a cup of hot chocolate while I explained about Ta-Na-E-Ka.

"Most amazing thing I ever heard," he said, when I was through. "I've lived next to the reservation all my life and this is the first I've heard of Ta-Na whatever-you-call-it." He looked at me, "Pretty silly thing to do to a kid," he muttered.

That was what I'd been thinking for months. But when Ernie said it, I became angry. "No, it *isn't* silly. It's a custom of the Kaw. We've been doing this for hundreds of years. My mother and my grandfather and everybody in my family went through this ceremony. It's why the Kaw are great warriors."

"Okay, great warrior," Ernie chuckled, "suit yourself. And, if you want to stick around, it's okay with me." Ernie went to the broom closet and tossed me a bundle. "That's the lost-and-found closet," he said. People leave stuff on boats. Maybe you'll find something to keep you warm."

The sweater fitted loosely, but it felt good. I felt good. And I'd found a new friend. Most important, I was surviving Ta-Na-E-Ka.

My grandfather had said the experience would be filled with adventure, and I was having my fill. And Grandfather never said we couldn't accept hospitality.

I stayed at Ernie's Riverside for the entire period. In the mornings I went into the woods and watched the animals and picked flowers for each of the tables in Ernie's. I had never felt better. I was up early enough to watch the sun rise on the Missouri, and I went to bed after it set. I ate everything I wanted—insisting that Ernie take all my money for the food. "I'll keep this in trust for you, Mary," Ernie promised, "in case you are ever desperate for five dollars."

I was sorry when the five days were over. I'd enjoyed every minute with Ernie. He taught me how to make western omelets and how to make Chili Ernie Style (still one of my favorite dishes). And I told Ernie all about the legends of the Kaw. I hadn't realized I knew so much about my people.

Ta-Na-E-Ka was over, and as I approached my house, at about nine-thirty in the evening, I became nervous all over again. What if Grandfather asked me about the berries and the grasshoppers? And my feet were hardly cut. I hadn't lost a pound and my hair was combed.

"They'll be so happy to see me," I told myself hopefully, "that they won't ask too many questions."

I opened the door. My grandfather was in the front room. He was wearing the beaded deerskin shirt which had belonged to *his* grandfather. "N'g'da'ma," he said. "Welcome back."

I embraced my parents warmly. I let go only when I saw my cousin Roger sprawled on the couch. His eyes were red and swollen. He'd lost weight. His feet were red and covered with blisters, and he was moaning, "I made it, see. I made it. I'm a warrior! A warrior!"

My grandfather looked at me strangely. I was clean, obviously well fed, and very healthy. My parents got the message. My uncle and aunt gazed at me.

Finally my grandfather asked, "What did you eat to keep you so well?"

I sucked in my breath and blurted out the truth, "Hamburgers and milk shakes."

"Hamburgers!" my grandfather growled.

"Milk shakes!" Roger moaned.

"You didn't say we *had* to eat grasshoppers," I said quietly, a little embarrassed.

"Tell us about your Ta-Na-E-Ka," my grandfather commanded.

I told them everything, from borrowing the five dollars, to Ernie's kindness.

"That's not what I trained you for," my grandfather said sadly.

I stood up. "Grandfather, I learned that Ta-Na-E-Ka *is* important. I didn't think so during training. I was scared stiff of it. I handled it my way. And I learned I had nothing to be afraid of. There's no reason today to eat grasshoppers when you can eat a hamburger."

I was shocked at my own boldness. But I liked it. "Grandfather, I'll bet you never ate one of those rotten berries yourself."

Grandfather laughed! He laughed aloud! My mother and father and aunt and uncle were all amazed. Grandfather never laughed! Never!

"Those berries—they are terrible," Grandfather admitted. "I could never swallow them. I found a dead deer on the first day of my Ta-Na-E-Ka—shot by a soldier, probably—and that kept my belly full for the entire period of the test!"

Grandfather stopped laughing. "We should send you out again," he said.

I looked at Roger. "You're pretty smart, Mary," Roger groaned. "I'd never have thought of what you did."

Roger tried to smile, but couldn't. My grandfather called me to him.

"You should have done what your cousin did," he said. "But I think you are more alert to what is happening to our people today than we are. I think you would have passed the test in any time. Somehow, you know how to exist in a world that wasn't made for Indians. I don't think you're going to have any trouble surviving."

Grandfather wasn't entirely right. But I'll tell about that another time.

Meet the Kaw

The Kaw, or Kansa Indians, lived west of the Mississippi River in what is now Kansas. In fact, both the state and the Kansas River take their name from *Kansa*, which means "people of the south wind." A proud people, who grew their own food and hunted buffalo, the Kaw were deeply devoted to family tradition, as "Ta-Na-E-Ka" suggests. As a result of smallpox and other diseases, their number has decreased over the years. Today most of the tribe lives in a small area in Osage County, Oklahoma, near Kansas. A celebrated Kaw tribal member was Charles Curtis, who served as vice president of the United States from 1929–1933. During his long career in Congress, he helped pass the Citizenship Act of 1924, which gave the right of United States citizenship to Native Americans.

Grandfather
by James K. Cazalas

It puzzles me
That I cannot see
What grandfather can:
He is eighty with the eyes
Of a young Indian   5
Proving his manhood.

I stumbled in the deep yellow sand
And he walked over it easily.
I breathed hard and perspired
And he paced himself   10
Like an animal
With a long way to go.

A dollar-sized turtle
Struggling on its back
Was dying ten feet off the sand: 15
It was he who saw it
And turned it over.

When we returned home,
He took off his sneakers,
Took out his teeth,   20
And was an old, dying man.
But on the trail
He was Seneca[1]
And more a part of the earth
Than the sand we trod.   25

1. *Seneca:* one of the five American Indian tribes that formed the powerful
   Iroquois nation.

YOU CAN ANSWER THESE QUESTIONS

Put an *x* in the box next to the correct answer.

Reading Comprehension

1. Kaw Indians took part in Ta-Na-E-Ka when they were
   - ❑ **a.** ten years old.
   - ❑ **b.** eleven years old.
   - ❑ **c.** fifteen years old.

2. Roger wanted to become
   - ❑ **a.** a great warrior.
   - ❑ **b.** a teacher.
   - ❑ **c.** an accountant.

3. Who was in charge of the training for Ta-Na-E-Ka?
   - ❑ **a.** Mary's mother
   - ❑ **b.** Mary's grandmother
   - ❑ **c.** Mary's grandfather

4. How much money did Mary borrow from Mrs. Richardson?
   - ❑ **a.** five dollars
   - ❑ **b.** fifteen dollars
   - ❑ **c.** twenty-five dollars

5. Where did Mary sleep during her Ta-Na-E-Ka?
   - ❑ **a.** in a boat
   - ❑ **b.** in a restaurant
   - ❑ **c.** in a forest

6. When Mary returned home after her Ta-Na-E-Ka, she looked
   - ❑ **a.** tired and thin.
   - ❑ **b.** sick and bruised.
   - ❑ **c.** clean, well fed, and healthy.

Vocabulary

7. "I don't want to be a warrior," Roger confided to Mary. The word *confided* means
   - ❑ **a.** told in secret.
   - ❑ **b.** wished for greatly.
   - ❑ **c.** walked away from.

8. When she returned home, Mary embraced her parents warmly. As used here, the word *embraced* means
   - ❑ **a.** warned.
   - ❑ **b.** hugged.
   - ❑ **c.** noticed.

9. Grandfather thought that Mary was alert to what was happening to their people. As used here, the word *alert* means
   - ❑ **a.** very aware.
   - ❑ **b.** not concerned about.
   - ❑ **c.** delighted with.

Idioms

10. When Mary complained about Ta-Na-E-Ka, she thought that Mrs. Richardson would take her side. When you *take someone's side*, you
    - ❑ **a.** argue with that person.
    - ❑ **b.** agree with that person.
    - ❑ **c.** hit that person in the side.

How many questions did you answer correctly? Circle your score. Then fill in your score on the Score Chart on page 184.

Number Correct	1	2	3	4	5	6	7	8	9	10
Score	10	20	30	40	50	60	70	80	90	100

EXERCISES TO HELP YOU

Exercise A

Understanding the story. Answer each question by writing a complete sentence. Be sure your sentences are grammatically correct. You may look back at the story.

1. At what age were Kaw Indians supposed to participate in Ta-Na-E-Ka?

   _____

   _____

2. What was Roger planning to be?

   _____

3. What impressed Mary about the Kaw?

   _____

   _____

4. How many days did Mary and Roger have to participate in Ta-Na-E-Ka?

   _____

   _____

5. Who was in charge of the training for Ta-Na-E-Ka?

   _____

6. How much money did Mrs. Richardson give Mary?

   _____

7. What did Mary eat for breakfast on her first day of Ta-Na-E-Ka?

   _____

8. Where did Mary stay during her entire Ta-Na-E-Ka?

   _____

9. How did Mary look when she returned home?

   _____

10. What did Grandfather eat during his Ta-Na-E-Ka?

    _____

    _____

Exercise B

Adding vocabulary. On the left are 10 words from the story. Complete each sentence by adding the correct word.

nourishing

heritage

survival

nightmares

participate

hospitality

dialect

sprawled

intention

protests

1. Ta-Na-E-Ka was the Kaw test of

   _____.

2. As Mary's birthday approached, she began to have

   awful _____ about it.

3. Although Grandfather spoke English, he used a

   Sioux _____ when he was with

   his family.

4. Mary had no _____ of remaining

   on the reservation for the rest of her life.

5. Although Mary complained, Mary's mother ignored

   her _____.

6. Mrs. Richardson told Mary not to "look down" on

   her _____.

7. Mary was nervous about it, but she knew that she

   would have to _____ in

   Ta-Na-E-Ka.

8. Grandfather said that berries tasted good and were

   very _____.

9. Mary accepted Ernie's _____ and

   stayed at the restaurant.

10. There, _____ on the couch,

    was her cousin, Roger.

Exercise C

Combining sentences by using adjective clauses. An **adjective clause** is a **subordinate clause** used as an adjective to modify a noun or a pronoun. Adjective clauses often begin with the **relative pronouns** *who, whom, which,* and *that.*

Combine each pair of sentences into one sentence that contains an adjective clause. Use the pronoun in parentheses. Write the sentence on the lines. The first one has been done for you.

1. Amos Deer Leg was a Kaw. He believed in tradition. (who)

   Amos Deer Leg was a Kaw who believed

   in tradition.

2. Roger was an eleven-year-old boy. He wanted to be an accountant. (who)

   _____

   _____

3. Mary Whitebird was the author. She wrote "Ta-Na-E-Ka." (who)

   _____

   _____

4. Mrs. Richardson was a teacher. Everyone admired her. (whom)

   _____

   _____

5. She gave her a five-dollar bill. It was new and crisp. (that)

   _____

   _____

6. Roger ate berries. He found them on the bushes. (that)

   _____

   _____

7. Ernie gave Mary a sweater. It fitted loosely. (that)

_____

_____

8. Mary looked at Roger's eyes. They were red and swollen. (which)

_____

_____

9. She ate hamburgers. They were delicious. (which)

_____

_____

10. Grandfather wore beaded moccasins. They were beautiful. (which)

_____

_____

Exercise D

Finding synonyms. Read the sentence. Then select the **synonym**
(the word most similar in meaning) for the word in capital letters. Circle
the letter of the correct answer. Each capitalized word appears in the story.

1. Ta-Na-E-Ka was a test of endurance.

    ENDURANCE   **a.** speed   **b.** strength   **c.** beauty

2. Only the strongest and smartest managed to survive.

    SURVIVE   **a.** live   **b.** help   **c.** complain

3. Mothers were not allowed to weep over a child who did not return.

    WEEP   **a.** cry   **b.** wonder   **c.** ask

4. Most Kaw legends were about "Good Woman," who led Kaw warriors
   into battle after battle.

    LEGENDS   **a.** pictures   **b.** stories   **c.** fights

5. Under the leadership of "Good Woman," the warriors were always
   victorious.

    VICTORIOUS   **a.** cautious   **b.** peaceful   **c.** triumphant

6. Mary and Roger went to separate "territories" and were not supposed
   to communicate with each other.

    COMMUNICATE   **a.** eat   **b.** work   **c.** talk

7. Grandfather demonstrated the way to eat a grasshopper.

    DEMONSTRATED   **a.** liked   **b.** learned   **c.** showed

8. Everyone said that for the next few days Mary and Roger would be
   dining on insects.

    DINING   **a.** catching   **b.** eating   **c.** worrying

9. Mary was unable to find a boat to sleep in. "There's not one boat here," she said dejectedly.

   DEJECTEDLY   **a.** cheerfully   **b.** sadly   **c.** hopefully

10. She suddenly realized that Ta-Na-E-Ka might be more fun than she had anticipated.

   ANTICIPATED   **a.** expected   **b.** wanted   **c.** needed

Exercise E

Understanding characters and plot. The following questions review **characters** and **plot** in a story. Fill in the box next to the correct answer.

1. Who is the main character in "Ta-Na-E-Ka"?
   - ❑ **a.** Grandfather
   - ❑ **b.** Mary
   - ❑ **c.** Roger

2. Select the sentence that best characterizes Mary.
   - ❑ **a.** She was independent and resourceful.
   - ❑ **b.** She was quiet and shy.
   - ❑ **c.** She was unable to handle new situations effectively.

3. How did Mary change during the course of the story?
   - ❑ **a.** She became convinced that the customs of the Kaw were very silly.
   - ❑ **b.** She lost confidence in her ability to succeed.
   - ❑ **c.** She learned to appreciate Ta-Na-E-Ka and her people.

4. At the end of the story, Grandfather
   - ❑ **a.** refused to forgive Mary for staying at the restaurant.
   - ❑ **b.** punished Mary by making her do her Ta-Na-E-Ka over again.
   - ❑ **c.** recognized that Mary had the skills she needed to survive in today's world.

5. What happened first in the plot of "Ta-Na-E-Ka"?
   - ❑ **a.** Grandfather asked Mary what she ate during her Ta-Na-E-Ka.
   - ❑ **b.** Mary and Roger kissed their parents and went off to the woods.
   - ❑ **c.** Mary told Ernie about Ta-Na-E-Ka.

6. What happened last in the plot of the story?
   - ❑ **a.** Ernie gave Mary a bundle of clothes.
   - ❑ **b.** Mary borrowed five dollars from Mrs. Richardson.
   - ❑ **c.** Grandfather revealed that he ate the meat from a deer on his Ta-Na-E-Ka.

7. Which one of the following played the most important part in the plot of the story?
   - ❑ **a.** Mary overslept on the floor of Ernie's Riverside restaurant.
   - ❑ **b.** When Roger returned home, his feet were red and sore.
   - ❑ **c.** Mary played on the riverbank and watched the birds.

Exercise F

Vocabulary review. Write a complete sentence for each word.

1. confided _____

_____

2. embraced _____

_____

3. hospitality _____

_____

4. nourishing _____

_____

5. participate _____

_____

6. survival _____

_____

7. nightmares _____

_____

8. heritage _____

_____

9. endurance _____

_____

10. legends _____

_____

SHARING WITH OTHERS

This section has been designed to provide you with opportunities to share your thoughts and ideas with others, while you practice and improve your reading, writing, speaking, and listening skills.

Part A

Discuss the following questions. Share your answers with your partner or with the group.

1. At the beginning of the story, Grandfather and Mary held different opinions about the value of Ta-Na-E-Ka. Whose opinion changed more during the course of the story—Grandfather's or Mary's? Explain why.

2. For months, Mary had been thinking that Ta-Na-E-Ka was pretty silly. However, when Ernie said so, Mary immediately became angry and defended the custom. Why do you think Mary acted the way she did?

3. In what ways was Mary's Ta-Na-E-Ka a valuable learning experience— for both Mary and Grandfather?

4. Do you think that Mary didn't "play by the rules" during her Ta-Na-E-Ka, or was she right to use any method available during her "test of survival"? Explain your reasoning.

5. If you were Grandfather, would you have made Mary do her Ta-Na-E-Ka over? Give reasons to support your answer.

6. Most families have certain customs or traditions. Describe a custom or tradition in your family. Tell how you feel about it. Is it a tradition you are likely to continue? Why?

Part B

Do you think that Ta-Na-E-Ka still serves a valuable purpose today, or do you believe that it has outlived its usefulness or may be too dangerous?

On the following lines, write a **persuasive composition** of at least 200 words. Explain why you think that Ta-Na-E-Ka should (or should *not*) be continued. State your point of view in the **introductory paragraph**. Present your arguments in the **body** of the composition. State your point of view again in the **concluding paragraph**.

_____

_____

_____

_____

_____

_____

_____

_____

_____

_____

_____

_____

_____

_____

_____

_____

_____

_____

_____

_____

_____

_____

_____

_____

_____

_____

_____

_____

_____

_____

_____

Part C
Poetry

GRANDFATHER

1. Why is the speaker puzzled by his grandfather? How can you explain the fact that Grandfather "sees" better and moves along the trail more easily than the much younger man?

2. Compare Grandfather on the trail and Grandfather at home.

3. In what ways is Grandfather in the poem similar to Grandfather in "Ta-Na-E-Ka"?

THE CIRCUIT

based on a story by Francisco Jiménez

Before You Read

Connections

Study the picture. Describe what you see.

- How old do you think the boy is? Is he happy or sad?
- Notice the boxes, the cooking pot, and the mattress. What is the boy doing at the top of the picture? What is he doing at the bottom of the picture?
- A *circuit* is a journey that a person repeats again and again. How might the title of the story be connected to what you see in the picture?
- Think about a time you moved to a new home. Describe the experience.

As you read, think about how the picture connects to the story.

Words to Learn

In this story, you will learn some new words. You will also learn some idioms. For example, *in store* is an idiom that means "in the future."

THE CIRCUIT

based on a story
by Francisco Jiménez

They worked twelve hours a day, seven days a week.

It was that time of year again. Ito, the strawberry sharecropper,[1] did not smile. It was natural. The peak of the strawberry season was over and the last few days the workers, most of them *braceros*,[2] were not picking as many boxes as they had during the months of June and July.

As the last days of August disappeared, so did the number of braceros. Sunday, only one—the best picker—came to work. I liked him. Sometimes we talked during our half-hour lunch break. That is how I found out he was from Jalisco, the same state in Mexico my family was from. That Sunday was the last time I saw him.

When the sun had tired and sunk behind the mountains, Ito signaled us that it was time to go home. "*Ya esora*,"[3] he yelled in his broken Spanish. Those were the words I waited for twelve hours a day, every day, seven days a week, week after week. And the thought of not hearing them again saddened me.

As we drove home Papa did not say a word. With both hands on the wheel, he stared at the dirt road. My older brother, Roberto, was also silent. He leaned his head back and closed his eyes. Once in a while he cleared from his throat the dust that blew in from outside.

Yes, it was that time of year. When I opened the front door to the shack, I stopped. Everything we owned was neatly packed in cardboard boxes. Suddenly I felt even more the weight of hours, days, weeks, and months of work. I sat down on a box. The thought

1. *sharecropper:* someone who works on a farm in return for a share of the crops.
2. *braceros:* Mexican farmworkers.
3. *Ya esora:* the Spanish phrase *ya es ora* means "it is time."

of having to move to Fresno and knowing what was in store for me there brought tears to my eyes.

That night I could not sleep. I lay in bed thinking about how much I hated this move.

A little before five o'clock in the morning, Papa woke everyone up. A few minutes later, the yelling and screaming of my little brothers and sisters, for whom the move was a great adventure, broke the silence of dawn. Shortly, the barking of the dogs accompanied them.

While we packed the breakfast dishes, Papa went outside to start the "Carcanchita." That was the name Papa gave his old '38 black Plymouth. He bought it in a used-car lot in Santa Rosa in the winter of 1949. Papa was very proud of his car. "*Mi Carcanchita,*" my little jalopy, he called it. He had a right to be proud of it. He spent a lot of time looking at other cars before buying this one. When he finally chose the "Carcanchita," he checked it thoroughly before driving it out of the car lot. He examined every inch of the car. He listened to the motor, tilting his head from side to side like a parrot, trying to detect any noises that spelled car trouble. After being satisfied with the looks and sounds of the car, Papa then insisted on knowing who the original owner was. He never did find out from the car salesman. But he bought the car anyway. Papa figured the original owner must have been an important man because behind the rear seat of the car he found a blue necktie.

Papa parked the car out in front and left the motor running. "*Listo*" (ready), he yelled. Without saying a word, Roberto and I began to carry the boxes out to the car. Roberto carried the two big boxes and I carried the two smaller ones. Papa then threw the mattress on top of the car roof and tied it with ropes to the front and rear bumpers.

Everything was packed except Mama's pot. It was an old large galvanized pot[4] she had picked up at an army surplus store in Santa Maria the year I was born. The pot was full of dents and nicks, and the more dents and nicks it had, the more Mama liked it. "*Mi olla*" (my pot), she used to say proudly.

I held the front door open as Mama carefully carried out her pot by both handles, making sure not to spill the cooked beans. When she got to the car, Papa reached out to help her with it. Roberto opened the rear car door and Papa gently placed it on the floor behind the front seat. All of us then climbed in. Papa sighed, wiped the sweat off his forehead with his sleeve, and said wearily: "*Es todo*" (that's it).

As we drove away, I felt a lump in my throat. I turned around and looked at our little shack for the last time.

At sunset we drove into a labor camp near Fresno. Since Papa did not speak English, Mama asked the camp foreman if he needed any more workers. "We don't need no more," said the foreman, scratching his head. "Check with Sullivan down the road. Can't miss him. He lives in a big white house with a fence around it."

When we got there, Mama walked up to the house. She went through a white gate, past a row of rose bushes, up the stairs to the front door. She rang the doorbell. The porch light went on and a tall husky man came out. They exchanged a few words. After the man went in, Mama clasped her hands and hurried back to the car. "We have work! Mr. Sullivan said we can stay there the whole season," she said gasping and pointing to an old garage near the stables.

The garage was worn out by the years. It had no windows. The walls, eaten by termites, strained to support the roof full of holes. The loose dirt floor, populated by earthworms, looked like a gray road map.

That night, by the light of a kerosene lamp, we unpacked and cleaned our new home. Roberto swept away the loose dirt, leaving the hard ground. Papa plugged the holes in the walls with old newspapers and tin can tops. Mama fed my little brothers and

---

4. *galvanized pot:* a pot that has been coated with a material to keep it from rusting.

sisters. Papa and Roberto then brought in the mattress and placed it on the far corner of the garage. "Mama, you and the little ones sleep on the mattress. Roberto, Panchito, and I will sleep outside under the trees," Papa said.

Early next morning Mr. Sullivan showed us where his crop was, and after breakfast, Papa, Roberto, and I headed for the vineyard to pick.

Around nine o'clock the temperature had risen to almost one hundred degrees. I was completely soaked in sweat and my mouth felt as if I had been chewing on a handkerchief. I walked over to the end of the row, picked up the jug of water we had brought, and began drinking. "Don't drink too much; you'll get sick," Roberto shouted. No sooner had he said that than I felt sick to my stomach. I dropped to my knees and let the jug roll off my hands. I remained motionless with my eyes glued on the hot sandy ground. All I could hear was the drone of insects. Slowly I began to recover. I poured water over my face and neck and watched the black mud run down my arms and hit the ground.

I still felt a little dizzy when we took a break to eat lunch. It was past two o'clock and we sat underneath a large walnut tree that was on the side of the road. While we ate, Papa jotted down the number of boxes we had picked. Roberto drew designs on the ground with a stick. Suddenly I noticed Papa's face turn pale as he looked down the road. "Here comes the school bus," he whispered loudly in alarm. Instinctively, Roberto and I ran and hid in the vineyards. We did not want to get in trouble for not going to school. The yellow bus stopped in front of Mr. Sullivan's house. Two neatly dressed boys about my age got off. They carried books under their arms. After they crossed the street, the bus drove away. Roberto and I came out from hiding and joined Papa. "*Tienen que tener cuidado*" (you have to be careful), he warned us.

After lunch we went back to work. The sun kept beating down. The buzzing insects, the wet sweat, and the hot dry dust made the afternoon seem to last forever. Finally the mountains around the valley reached out and swallowed the sun. Within an hour it was too dark to continue picking. The vines blanketed the grapes, making it difficult to see the bunches. "*Vámonos*,"[5] said Papa, signaling to us that it was time to quit work. Papa then took out a pencil and began to figure out how much we had earned our first day. He wrote down numbers, crossed some out, wrote down some more. "*Quince*" (fifteen dollars), he murmured.

When we arrived home, we took a cold shower underneath a waterhose. We then sat down to eat dinner around some wooden crates that served as a table. Mama had cooked a special meal for us. We had rice and tortillas with *carne con chile*, my favorite dish.

The next morning I could hardly move. My body ached all over. I felt little control over my arms and legs. This feeling went on every morning for days until my muscles finally got used to the work.

It was Monday, the first week of November. The grape season was over and I could now go to school. I woke up early that morning and lay in bed, looking at the stars and savoring the thought of not going to work and of starting sixth grade for the first time that year. Since I could not sleep, I decided to get up and join Papa and Roberto at breakfast. I sat at the table across from Roberto, but I kept my head down. I did not want to look up and face him. I knew he was sad. He was not going to school today. He was not going tomorrow, or next week, or next month. He would not go until the cotton season was over, and that was sometime in February. I rubbed my hands together and watched the dry, acid-stained skin fall to the floor in little rolls.

When Papa and Roberto left for work, I felt relief. I walked to the top of a small grade next to the shack and watched the "Carcanchita" disappear in the distance in a cloud of dust.

Two hours later, around eight o'clock, I stood by the side of the

5. *Vámonos:* Let's go.

road waiting for school bus number twenty. When it arrived I climbed in. No one noticed me. Everyone was busy either talking or yelling. I sat in an empty seat in the back.

When the bus stopped in front of the school, I felt very nervous. I looked out the bus window and saw boys and girls carrying books under their arms. I felt empty. I put my hands in my pants pockets and walked to the principal's office. When I entered I heard a woman's voice say: "May I help you?" I was startled. I had not heard English for months. For a few seconds I remained speechless. I looked at the lady who waited for an answer.

My first instinct was to answer her in Spanish, but I held back. Finally, after struggling for English words I managed to tell her that I wanted to enroll in the sixth grade. After answering many questions, I was led to the classroom.

Mr. Lema, the sixth-grade teacher, greeted me and assigned me a desk. He then introduced me to the class. I was so nervous and scared at that moment when everyone's eyes were on me that I wished I were with Papa and Roberto picking cotton. After taking roll, Mr. Lema gave the class the assignment for the first hour. "The first thing we have to do this morning is finish reading the story we began yesterday," he said enthusiastically. He walked up to me, handed me an English book, and asked me to read. "We are on page 125," he said politely. When I heard this, I felt my blood rush to my head; I felt dizzy. "Would you like to read?" he asked hesitantly. I opened the book to page 125. My mouth was dry. My eyes began to water. I could not begin. "You can read later," Mr. Lema said understandingly.

For the rest of the reading period I kept getting angrier and angrier with myself. I should have read, I thought to myself.

During recess I went into the restroom and opened my English book to page 125. I began to read in a low voice, pretending I was in class. There were many words I did not know. I closed the book and headed back to the classroom.

Mr. Lema was sitting at his desk correcting papers. When I entered he looked up at me and smiled. I felt better. I walked up to him and asked if he could help me with the new words. "Gladly," he said.

The rest of the month I spent my lunch hours working on English with Mr. Lema, my best friend at school.

One Friday during lunch hour Mr. Lema asked me to take a walk with him to the music room. "Do you like music?" he asked me as we entered the building.

"Yes, I like Mexican *corridos*,"[6] I answered. He then picked up a trumpet, blew on it and handed it to me. The sound gave me goose bumps. I knew that sound. I had heard it in many Mexican corridos. "How would you like to learn how to play it?" he asked. He must have read my face because before I could answer, he added: "I'll teach you how to play it during our lunch hours."

That day I could hardly wait to get home to tell Papa and Mama the great news. As I got off the bus, my little brothers and sisters ran up to meet me. They were yelling and screaming. I thought they were happy to see me, but when I opened the door to our shack, I saw that everything we owned was neatly packed in cardboard boxes.

Meet the Author

Francisco Jiménez was born in Jalisco, Mexico, and immigrated to California with his family when he was four years old. "The Circuit," based on the author's experiences growing up in California, was written in Spanish and then translated into English. When it was published in 1973, it won The Arizona Quarterly Annual Award. The author earned a doctorate from Columbia University in New York and now teaches Spanish language and literature at the University of Santa Clara in California. He has written and edited many articles and short stories.

6. *corridos:* popular songs; ballads.

YOU CAN ANSWER THESE QUESTIONS

Put an *x* in the box next to the correct answer.

Reading Comprehension

1. At the beginning of the story, Panchito was sad because he
   - ❏ **a.** hadn't seen his family for a long time.
   - ❏ **b.** didn't want to move to Fresno.
   - ❏ **c.** was feeling ill.

2. How did Papa feel about his used car?
   - ❏ **a.** He was very proud of it.
   - ❏ **b.** He was ashamed of it.
   - ❏ **c.** He didn't care about it.

3. Mr. Sullivan said that the family could stay
   - ❏ **a.** in a big white house.
   - ❏ **b.** with some friends who lived nearby.
   - ❏ **c.** in a garage.

4. How much did the family earn the first day on the new job?
   - ❏ **a.** ten dollars
   - ❏ **b.** fifteen dollars
   - ❏ **c.** twenty dollars

5. Why didn't Panchito read to the class on his first day at school?
   - ❏ **a.** He was too nervous to read.
   - ❏ **b.** He didn't understand any of the words
   - ❏ **c.** He didn't have a book.

6. Mr. Lema said that he would teach Panchito how to play
   - ❏ **a.** the piano.
   - ❏ **b.** the trumpet.
   - ❏ **c.** the violin.

7. At the end of the story, Panchito discovered that
   - ❏ **a.** Mr. Lema had a new job.
   - ❏ **b.** the family had to leave in a month.
   - ❏ **c.** everything they owned was packed in boxes.

Vocabulary

8. He tried to detect if there was anything wrong with the car. The word *detect* means
   - ❏ **a.** stop.
   - ❏ **b.** watch.
   - ❏ **c.** discover.

9. Papa asked, "Who was the original owner of the car?" The word *original* means
   - ❏ **a.** first.
   - ❏ **b.** last.
   - ❏ **c.** best.

Idioms

10. He knew what was in store for him in Fresno, so he wanted to stay home. The idiom *in store* means
    - ❏ **a.** in a grocery store.
    - ❏ **b.** in a shop.
    - ❏ **c.** in the future.

How many questions did you answer correctly? Circle your score. Then fill in your score on the Score Chart on page 184.

Number Correct	1	2	3	4	5	6	7	8	9	10
Score	10	20	30	40	50	60	70	80	90	100

EXERCISES TO HELP YOU

Exercise A

Understanding the story. Answer each question by writing a complete sentence. Be sure your sentences are grammatically correct. You may look back at the story.

1. Where was the family moving to at the beginning of "The Circuit"?

   _____

   _____

2. What did Papa find behind a seat in the car?

   _____

   _____

3. How long did Mr. Sullivan say the family could stay?

   _____

   _____

4. Where did the family live when they worked for Mr. Sullivan?

   _____

   _____

5. Where did Roberto, Panchito, and Papa sleep?

   _____

   _____

6. How much did the family earn their first day on the new job?

   _____

   _____

7. Why was Panchito able to go to school in November?

_____

_____

_____

8. What grade was Panchito in at school?

_____

_____

9. How did Panchito spend his lunch hour at school?

_____

_____

10. At the end of the story, what did Panchito see when he opened the door?

_____

_____

Exercise B

Adding vocabulary. On the left are 10 words from the story. Complete each sentence by adding the correct word.

vineyard

dawn

pretending

enroll

populated

husky

crates

muscles

peak

instinct

1. Everyone got up at five o'clock in the morning, and the family was ready to leave by _____.

2. Since the _____ of the season was over, some of the workers had left.

3. Mama rang the bell and a tall, _____ man came to the door.

4. The ground was covered with earth, which was _____ by worms.

5. Papa, Roberto, and Panchito began to pick grapes in the _____.

6. Panchito ached all over until his _____ finally got used to the work.

7. They ate dinner on wooden _____ that served as a table.

8. When Panchito arrived at school, he explained that he wanted to _____ in the sixth grade.

9. Although Panchito's first _____ was to speak Spanish, he answered in English.

10. He read softly in the restroom, _____ that he was in class.

Exercise C

Part A

Combining sentences. Combine two **simple sentences** into one **complex sentence** by using the **subordinating conjunction** in parentheses. Begin the sentence with the conjunction, and use a comma at the end of the **clause**. Write the complex sentence on the line. The first one has been done for you.

Common Subordinating Conjunctions

after	since	as	when
although	though	if	while

1. The strawberry season was over. The family had to move. (since)

   Since the strawberry season was over, the family had to move.

2. The car was very old. Papa liked it very much. (although)

   _____

   _____

3. Papa packed the car. Mama prepared food for the trip. (while)

   _____

   _____

4. The family drove away. Panchito looked back at their little shack. (as)

   _____

   _____

5. The work was very hard. Panchito got used to it. (though)

   _____

   _____

6. Panchito entered the classroom. Mr. Lema introduced him to the class. (after)

   _____

   _____

7. You can come here during your lunch hour. I will help you with your English. (if)

_____

_____

8. Panchito studied every day. His English improved rapidly. (since)

_____

_____

9. Panchito opened the door. He saw the boxes on the floor. (when)

_____

_____

Part B

Combine two **simple sentences** into one **complex sentence** by using the **subordinating conjunctions** below. Begin the sentence with the conjunction, and use a comma at the end of the clause. Write the complex sentence on the line. Use each conjunction once.

after   although   since   while

10. Papa didn't speak English. Mama spoke to Mr. Sullivan.

_____

_____

11. Roberto swept the floor of the garage. Papa was fixing the walls.

_____

_____

12. Roberto wanted to go to school now. He had to wait until February.

_____

_____

13. Panchito drank too much water. He felt sick.

_____

_____

Exercise D

Finding synonyms. Read the sentence. Then select the **synonym** (the word most similar in meaning) for the word in capital letters. Circle the letter of the correct answer. Each capitalized word appears in the story.

1. Papa checked the car thoroughly before driving it out of the lot.

    THOROUGHLY   **a.** quickly   **b.** carefully   **c.** quietly

2. He listened to the motor, tilting his head from side to side.

    TILTING   **a.** leaning   **b.** hearing   **c.** keeping

3. Panchito lay in bed looking at the stars and savoring the thought of not going to work.

    SAVORING   **a.** watching   **b.** hating   **c.** enjoying

4. Papa plugged the holes in the walls with old newspapers.

    PLUGGED   **a.** emptied   **b.** filled   **c.** broke

5. The only thing that Panchito could hear was the drone of insects.

    DRONE   **a.** humming   **b.** work   **c.** wings

6. His father took a pencil and jotted down the number of boxes they had filled.

    JOTTED   **a.** carried   **b.** wrote   **c.** read

7. He had not heard English for so long, he was startled when she said, "May I help you?"

    STARTLED   **a.** saddened   **b.** bothered   **c.** surprised

8. She waited for him to answer, but he was speechless.

    SPEECHLESS   **a.** silent   **b.** lost   **c.** pleased

9. The teacher, Mr. Lema, greeted Panchito and assigned him a seat.

    ASSIGNED   **a.** gave   **b.** needed   **c.** demanded

10. "You're sure to enjoy the story we began reading yesterday," he said enthusiastically.

    ENTHUSIASTICALLY   **a.** shyly   **b.** angrily   **c.** eagerly

Exercise E

Thinking critically. How well did you "read between the lines"? The following questions will help you read critically. Fill in the box next to the correct answer.

1. The last sentence of "The Circuit" suggests that
   - ❏ **a.** the shack was too small for the family.
   - ❏ **b.** the family owned many things.
   - ❏ **c.** the family was about to move again.

2. When Panchito saw the boxes at the end of the story, he probably felt
   - ❏ **a.** pleased.
   - ❏ **b.** shocked and sad.
   - ❏ **c.** quite calm.

3. Which statement is true?
   - ❏ **a.** The family worked hard and long for very little money.
   - ❏ **b.** The family lived in Mexico.
   - ❏ **c.** The family usually worked in the same place all year.

4. The mother probably spent most of her time
   - ❏ **a.** working in the fields with her husband.
   - ❏ **b.** driving the Carcanchita.
   - ❏ **c.** cooking and taking care of her youngest children.

5. "The Circuit" is a true story. We may infer that the author was
   - ❏ **a.** Papa.
   - ❏ **b.** Mama.
   - ❏ **c.** Panchito.

Exercise F
Vocabulary review. Write a complete sentence for each word.

1. detect _____

   _____

2. original _____

   _____

3. enroll _____

   _____

4. husky _____

   _____

5. populated _____

   _____

6. crates _____

   _____

7. savoring _____

   _____

8. dawn _____

   _____

9. instinct _____

   _____

10. pretending _____

    _____

Sharing with Others

This section has been designed to provide you with opportunities to share your thoughts and ideas with others, while you practice and improve your reading, writing, speaking, and listening skills.

Part A

Discuss the following questions. Share your answers with your partner or with the group.

1. Why was it necessary for the family to move from place to place? What were some of the hardships the family had to endure? What strengths and qualities did the family possess that helped them deal with the difficulties they encountered?

2. On the morning that Panchito left for school, he could not look at his brother's face at breakfast. Why?

3. Point out the various ways in which Mr. Lema helped Panchito and tried to make him feel more comfortable at school. How do you know that Panchito was a very enthusiastic student?

4. At the end of the story, Panchito rushed home from school to tell his family "the great news." However, when he opened the door, he saw that everything they owned was neatly packed in cardboard boxes. Explain how this incident makes the conclusion of the story sadder and more powerful.

5. Look up the word *circuit* in the dictionary. If possible, also search the Internet for *circuit* as it relates to migrant workers in the western United States. Then explain why "The Circuit" is such an appropriate title for the story. Give at least two reasons.

6. When Panchito arrived at the school, his first instinct was to speak Spanish. However, he "held back" and struggled in English. Have you ever experienced a time when you felt that your English was weak, but you "struggled through"? Tell what happened.

Part B

"The Circuit" is an **autobiographical** story. This means it is based on events that took place in the writer's life. Mr. Lema was actually the author's teacher, one of three teachers who changed the course of Mr. Jiménez's life.

Suppose that years after leaving Fresno, Panchito decided to write a letter to Mr. Lema. What do you think Panchito might say?

On the lines below, write Panchito's letter. You will probably want to refer to your first day at school and to the strong influence that Mr. Lema had on you.

Dear Mr. Lema,

_____

_____

_____

_____

_____

_____

_____

_____

_____

_____

_____

_____

_____

_____

_____

Your friend,

Panchito

A BOY'S BEST FRIEND

based on a story by Isaac Asimov

Before You Read

Connections

Study the picture on the left. Describe what you see.

- Where and when does this story take place? How do you know?
- What does the robot look like? Does the boy like the robot? What clues tell you?
- Who or what do you think is "a boy's best friend"?
- What do you think will happen to the boy and the robot in the story?
- Do you have a pet that is a special friend to you, or do you know someone who does? Tell why the pet is special.

As you read, think about how the picture connects to the story.

Words to Learn

In this story, you will learn some new words. You will also learn some idioms. For example, *show off* means "show how well you can do something."

A Boy's Best Friend

based on a story by Isaac Asimov

The boy already had a best friend.

Mr. Anderson said, "Where's Jimmy, dear?"

"He's out on the crater,"[1] said Mrs. Anderson. "He'll be all right. Robutt is with him.—Did he arrive?"

"Yes. He's at the rocket station, going through the tests. Actually, I can hardly wait to see him myself. I haven't really seen one since I left Earth fifteen years ago. You can't count pictures."

"Jimmy has *never* seen one," said Mrs. Anderson.

"That's because he's Moonborn and can't visit Earth. That's why I'm bringing one here. I think it's the first dog anyone has ever seen on the Moon."

"It cost enough," said Mrs. Anderson, with a small sigh.

"Maintaining[2] Robutt isn't cheap, either," said Mr. Anderson.

Jimmy was out on the crater, as his mother had said. By Earth standards, he was thin, but rather tall for a ten-year-old. His arms and legs were long and agile.[3] He looked thicker and heavier with his spacesuit on, but he could handle the lunar gravity as no Earthborn human being could. His father couldn't begin to keep up with him when Jimmy stretched his legs and went into the kangaroo hop.

The outer side of the crater sloped southward and the Earth, which was low in the southern sky (where it always was, as seen from Lunar City), was nearly full, so that the entire crater-slope was brightly lit.

1. *crater:* a wide hole or valley on the moon.
2. *maintaining:* keeping in good condition.
3. *agile:* able to move very quickly and easily.

The slope was a gentle one and even the weight of the spacesuit couldn't keep Jimmy from racing up it in a floating hop that made the gravity seem nonexistent.

"Come on, Robutt," he shouted.

Robutt, who could hear him by radio, squeaked and bounded after him.

Jimmy, expert though he was, couldn't outrace Robutt, who didn't need a spacesuit, and had four legs and tendons of steel. Robutt sailed over Jimmy's head, somersaulting and landing almost under his feet.

"Don't show off, Robutt," said Jimmy, "and stay in sight."

Robutt squeaked again, the special squeak that meant "Yes."

"I don't trust you, you faker," shouted Jimmy, and up he went in one last bound that carried him over the curved upper edge of the crater wall and down onto the inner slope.

The Earth sank below the top of the crater wall and at once it was pitch-dark around him. A warm, friendly darkness that wiped out the difference between ground and sky except for the glitter of stars.

Actually, Jimmy wasn't supposed to exercise along the dark side of the crater wall. The grown-ups said it was dangerous, but that was because they were never there. The ground was smooth and crunchy, and Jimmy knew the exact location of every one of the few rocks.

Besides, how could it be dangerous racing through the dark when *Robutt* was right there with him, bouncing around and squeaking and glowing? Even without the glow, Robutt could tell where he was, and where Jimmy was, by radar. Jimmy couldn't go wrong while Robutt was around, tripping him when he was too near a rock, or jumping on him to show how much he loved him, or circling around and squeaking low and scared when Jimmy hid behind a rock, when all the time Robutt knew well enough where he was. Once Jimmy had pretended he was hurt and Robutt had sounded the radio alarm and people from Lunar City got there in a hurry. Jimmy's father had let him hear about *that* little trick, and Jimmy never tried it again.

Just as he was remembering that, he heard his father's voice on his private wavelength. "Jimmy, come back. I have something to tell you."

Jimmy was out of his spacesuit now and washed up. You always had to wash up after coming in from outside. Even Robutt had to be sprayed, but he loved it. He stood there on all fours, his little foot-long body quivering and glowing just a tiny bit, and his small head, with no mouth, with two large glass eyes, and with a bump where the brain was. He squeaked until Mr. Anderson said, "Quiet, Robutt."

Mr. Anderson was smiling. "We have something for you, Jimmy. It's at the rocket station now, but we'll have it tomorrow after all the tests are over. I thought I'd tell you now."

"From Earth, Dad?"

"A *dog* from Earth, son. A *real* dog! A Scotch terrier puppy. The first dog on the Moon. You won't need Robutt anymore. We can't keep them both, you know, and some other boy or girl will have Robutt." Dad seemed to be waiting for Jimmy to say something, then he said, "You know what a dog is, Jimmy. It's the *real* thing. Robutt's only a mechanical imitation, a robot-mutt. That's how he got his name."

Jimmy frowned. "Robutt isn't an imitation, Dad. He's my dog."

"He's not a real one, Jimmy. Robutt's just steel and wiring and a simple computer brain. It's not *alive*."

"He does everything I want him to do, Dad. He understands me. Sure, he's alive."

"No, son. Robutt is just a machine. It's just programmed to act the way it does. A dog *is* alive. You won't want Robutt after you have the dog."

"The dog will need a spacesuit, won't he?"

"Yes, of course. But it will be worth the money and he'll get used to it. And he won't need one in the City. You'll see the difference once he gets here."

Jimmy looked at Robutt, who was squeaking again, a very low, slow squeak, that seemed frightened. Jimmy held out his arms and Robutt was in them in one bound. Jimmy said, "What will the difference be between Robutt and the dog?"

"It's hard to explain," said Mr. Anderson, "but it will be easy to see. The dog will *really* love you. Robutt is just programmed to act as though it loves you."

"But, Dad, we don't know what's *inside* the dog, or what his feelings are. Maybe it's just acting, too."

Mr. Anderson frowned. "Jimmy, you'll *know* the difference when you experience the love of a living thing."

Jimmy held Robutt tightly. Jimmy was frowning, too, and the desperate look on his face meant that he wouldn't change his mind. He said, "But what's the difference how *they* act? How about how *I* feel? I love Robutt and *that's* what counts."

And the little robot-mutt, which had never been held so tightly in all its existence, squeaked high and rapid squeaks—happy squeaks!

Meet the Author

Isaac Asimov (*1920–1992*) was born in Russia and came to the United States with his family when he was three years old. As a young boy he saw a science-fiction magazine on a rack in his father's store, and that sparked the beginning of an amazingly productive writing career. In fact, Asimov wrote so many books and short stories that even he lost track of the number. His books alone, on a wide variety of subjects, number over four hundred. Asimov earned his Ph.D. at Columbia University. He taught at several colleges and wrote dozens of textbooks and scientific articles. However, he is best known for his science-fiction novels. Among his most popular are *I Robot*, *The Robots of Dawn*, and *The Foundation Trilogy*.

Moco Limping
by David Nava Monreal

My dog hobbles[1]
with a stick
of a leg that
he drags behind
him as he moves.   5
And I was a man
that wanted a
beautiful, noble
animal as a pet.
I wanted him   10
to be strong and
capture all the
attention by
the savage grace
of his gait.[2]   15
I wanted him to
be the first
dog howling in
the pack.
The leader,   20
the brutal hunter
that broke through
the woods with
thunder.
But, instead he's   25
this rickety[3]
little canine[4]
that leaves trails
in the dirt
with his club foot.[5]   30

1. *hobbles:* walks in an unusual way; walks with a limp.
2. *gait:* way of walking.
3. *rickety:* weak and shaky.
4. *canine:* dog.
5. *club foot:* a foot that has not grown correctly. It is usually short and
   may have an unusual shape.

He's the stumbler
that trips while
chasing lethargic[6]
bees and butterflies.
It hurts me to   35
see him so
abnormal,
so clumsy and
stupid.
My vain heart weeps   40
knowing he
is mine.
But then he turns
my way and
looks at me with   45
eyes that cry out
with life.
He jumps at me with
his feeble paws.
I feel his warm fur   50
and his imperfection[7] is
        forgotten.

6. *lethargic:* slow moving; lazy.
7. *imperfection:* As used here, the word means "fault."

YOU CAN ANSWER THESE QUESTIONS

Put an *x* in the box next to the correct answer.

Reading Comprehension

1. Mr. Anderson left Earth
   - ❏ **a.** ten years ago.
   - ❏ **b.** fifteen years ago.
   - ❏ **c.** twenty years ago.

2. Jimmy was playing
   - ❏ **a.** at the rocket station.
   - ❏ **b.** on the crater.
   - ❏ **c.** in his backyard.

3. When Jimmy got too near a rock, Robutt would
   - ❏ **a.** trip him.
   - ❏ **b.** bark.
   - ❏ **c.** send an alarm.

4. Select the sentence that best describes Robutt.
   - ❏ **a.** He had a small head, no mouth, and two glass eyes.
   - ❏ **b.** He was made of steel and was three feet long.
   - ❏ **c.** He was a Scotch terrier puppy.

5. Select the statement that is not true.
   - ❏ **a.** Dad said they couldn't keep Robutt and the dog.
   - ❏ **b.** Dad said that Jimmy wouldn't want Robutt after Jimmy got a real dog.
   - ❏ **c.** Jimmy was thrilled to get a dog from Earth.

6. What was most important to Jimmy?
   - ❏ **a.** getting a real dog
   - ❏ **b.** visiting Earth
   - ❏ **c.** keeping Robutt

Vocabulary

7. Jimmy frowned when Dad said they would have to give Robutt away. The word *frowned* means
   - ❏ **a.** looked happy.
   - ❏ **b.** looked unhappy.
   - ❏ **c.** looked interested.

Idioms

8. The rescuers got to Jimmy in a hurry. The idiom *in a hurry* means
   - ❏ **a.** very worried.
   - ❏ **b.** very quickly.
   - ❏ **c.** very carefully.

9. Jimmy told Robutt, "Don't show off." When you *show off*, you show
   - ❏ **a.** how well you can do something.
   - ❏ **b.** that you are shy.
   - ❏ **c.** that you are helpful.

10. Jimmy began to run; his father couldn't keep up with him. As used here, the idiom *keep up with* means
    - ❏ **a.** call to.
    - ❏ **b.** pay for.
    - ❏ **c.** move as fast as.

How many questions did you answer correctly? Circle your score. Then fill in your score on the Score Chart on page 184.

Number Correct	1	2	3	4	5	6	7	8	9	10
Score	10	20	30	40	50	60	70	80	90	100

Exercise A

Understanding the story. Answer each question by writing a complete sentence. Be sure your sentences are grammatically correct. You may look back at the story.

1. Where was Jimmy playing?

    _____

    _____

2. Where was the dog that Mr. Anderson was planning to give Jimmy?

    _____

    _____

3. Who was with Jimmy?

    _____

    _____

4. How long ago had Mr. Anderson left Earth?

    _____

    _____

5. Who could run faster—Jimmy or Robutt?

    _____

    _____

6. What did Robutt do when Jimmy got too near a rock?

    _____

    _____

7. What happened one time when Jimmy pretended he was hurt?

_____

_____

8. What two things did Jimmy do when he came in from outside?

_____

_____

9. Why didn't Jimmy want a new dog?

_____

_____

10. How did Robutt feel at the end of the story?

_____

_____

Exercise B

Adding vocabulary. On the left are 10 words from the story. Complete each sentence by adding the correct word.

imitation

gravity

tendons

somersaulting

agile

standards

programmed

sloped

radar

outrace

1. By Earth _____, Jimmy was thin and rather tall.

2. Jimmy's arms and legs were long and _____.

3. Jimmy could handle the moon's _____ better than anyone who was born on Earth.

4. One side of the crater _____ to the south.

5. Robutt's legs were made of metal, and he had _____ of steel.

6. Although Jimmy was a very fast runner, he couldn't _____ Robutt.

7. Robutt sailed over Jimmy's head, _____ and landing near his feet.

8. Robutt knew exactly where Jimmy was because Robutt was equipped with _____.

9. According to Jimmy's father, Robutt wasn't a real dog; it was only an _____.

10. Robutt was a machine that was _____ to act the way it did.

Exercise C

Direct quotations and reported speech. Change the direct quotations to reported speech by using the word *if*. Make the necessary changes in tense and pronouns. Write the sentences on the lines. The first one has been done for you.

1. Mr. Anderson asked, "Is Jimmy on the crater?"

Mr. Anderson asked if Jimmy was on the crater.

2. Mrs. Anderson asked, "Did the dog arrive?"

3. Mr. Anderson wondered, "Is Jimmy safe?"

4. Jimmy wondered, "Do people still live on Earth?"

5. Mom asked, "Did you have fun with Robutt?"

6. Dad asked Jimmy, "Don't you want a real dog?"

7. Jimmy asked, "Will the dog need a spacesuit?"

Exercise D

Finding synonyms. Read the sentence. Then select the **synonym** (the word most similar in meaning) for the word in capital letters. Circle the letter of the correct answer. Each capitalized word appears in the story.

1. Since Jimmy was Moonborn, he was used to lunar life.

   LUNAR   **a.** earth   **b.** moon   **c.** sun

2. As soon as Robutt heard Jimmy's voice, it bounded after him.

   BOUNDED   **a.** watched   **b.** cried   **c.** jumped

3. Jimmy knew where Robutt was because Jimmy could see him glowing.

   GLOWING   **a.** waving   **b.** shining   **c.** calling

4. Except for the glitter of stars, there was darkness everywhere.

   GLITTER   **a.** sparkle   **b.** noise   **c.** darkness

5. Jimmy hopped in a way that made gravity seem nonexistent.

   NONEXISTENT   **a.** alive   **b.** absent   **c.** field

6. After they washed Robutt, he stood there quivering.

   QUIVERING   **a.** shaking   **b.** thinking   **c.** laughing

7. Jimmy heard Robutt's special squeak; Jimmy knew it meant "Yes."

   SQUEAK   **a.** radio   **b.** power   **c.** sound

8. Robutt was mechanical; it was made of steel and had a computer for a brain.

   MECHANICAL   **a.** machinery   **b.** friendly   **c.** real

Exercise E

Understanding the setting of a story. The **setting** of a story is *where* and *when* the main action takes place. How well did you understand the setting of "A Boy's Best Friend"? Fill in the box next to the correct answer.

1. Where is the story set?
   - ❏ **a.** on Earth
   - ❏ **b.** on the Moon
   - ❏ **c.** on a distant star

2. When does "A Boy's Best Friend" take place?
   - ❏ **a.** in the past
   - ❏ **b.** at the present time
   - ❏ **c.** in the future

3. Because of the setting, it was necessary for Jimmy to
   - ❏ **a.** wear a spacesuit.
   - ❏ **b.** have a pet.
   - ❏ **c.** eat very little.

4. You "always had to wash up after coming in from outside. Even Robutt had to be sprayed." This suggests that
   - ❏ **a.** Jimmy and Robutt always got very dirty when they played outside.
   - ❏ **b.** there may have been something harmful on the surface or in the atmosphere.
   - ❏ **c.** Jimmy's parents wanted Jimmy and Robutt to look clean all the time.

5. Why was Jimmy able to hop and jump through the air so easily?
   - ❏ **a.** He was very powerful.
   - ❏ **b.** He weighed very little.
   - ❏ **c.** The pull of gravity there was not very strong.

Exercise F

Vocabulary review. Write a complete sentence for each word or group of words.

1. frowned _____

_____

2. imitation _____

_____

3. gravity _____

_____

4. agile _____

_____

5. radar _____

_____

6. sloped _____

_____

7. mechanical _____

_____

8. quivering _____

_____

9. in a hurry _____

_____

10. keep up with _____

_____

SHARING WITH OTHERS

This section has been designed to provide you with opportunities to share your thoughts and ideas with others, while you practice and improve your reading, writing, speaking, and listening skills.

Part A

Discuss the following questions. Share your answers with your partner or with the group.

1. How did Mr. Anderson expect Jimmy to react to the news that he was about to receive a dog from Earth? How *did* Jimmy react? Why?

2. As long as Robutt was with Jimmy, Mr. and Mrs. Anderson were not concerned that Jimmy was playing on a dangerous crater. Explain why.

3. The dog from Earth was at the rocket station, going through tests. What tests do you suppose those were, and why was it necessary for the dog to take them?

4. The dog from Earth would need a spacesuit. Why? Why didn't Robutt also need a spacesuit?

5. In many ways, Robutt was like a real dog. For example, when Mr. Anderson said, "Quiet," Robutt obeyed his command. Find other examples of ways in which Robutt acted just like a real dog. Why do you think the author provided these incidents?

6. Do you think that the Andersons will insist that Jimmy keep the new dog? Why? If so, do you think that Jimmy will eventually grow to love the dog from Earth? Explain your answer.

7. Why is the story called "A Boy's Best Friend"? Think of another interesting and appropriate title.

Part B

Robutt was a machine that was programmed to act as though it were alive. That raises this interesting question: Can machines think? Before you answer, consider the following: Airplanes can fly, although they do not flap their wings like birds. And computers are capable of beating people at chess. Still, can a machine write a great novel or poem? Can it appreciate and discuss the acting in a play?

Write a **composition** explaining why you think that machines can (or cannot) think. State your point of view in the **introductory paragraph**. In the **body** of the composition, present examples and illustrations to support your point of view. In the **concluding paragraph**, state your point of view again.

Part C
Poetry

MOCO LIMPING

1. What kind of a dog does the speaker want? Why is the speaker disappointed in his dog? Why does the speaker forget about his dog's "imperfection"?

2. What expressions in the poem strike you as particularly moving or powerful?

3. In what ways is Moco similar to Robutt? How are they different?

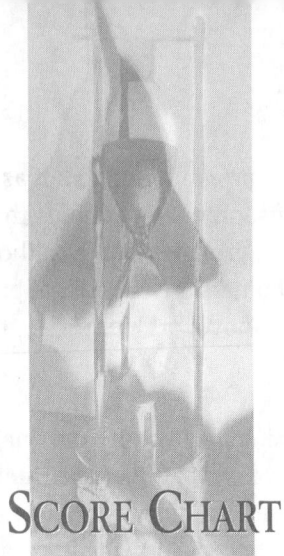

SCORE CHART

This is the Score Chart for YOU CAN ANSWER THESE QUESTIONS.
Shade in your score for each part of the story. For example, if your
score was 80 for **The Teacher**, look at the bottom of the chart for
The Teacher. Shade in the bar up to the 80 mark. By looking at this
chart, you can see how well you did on each story.

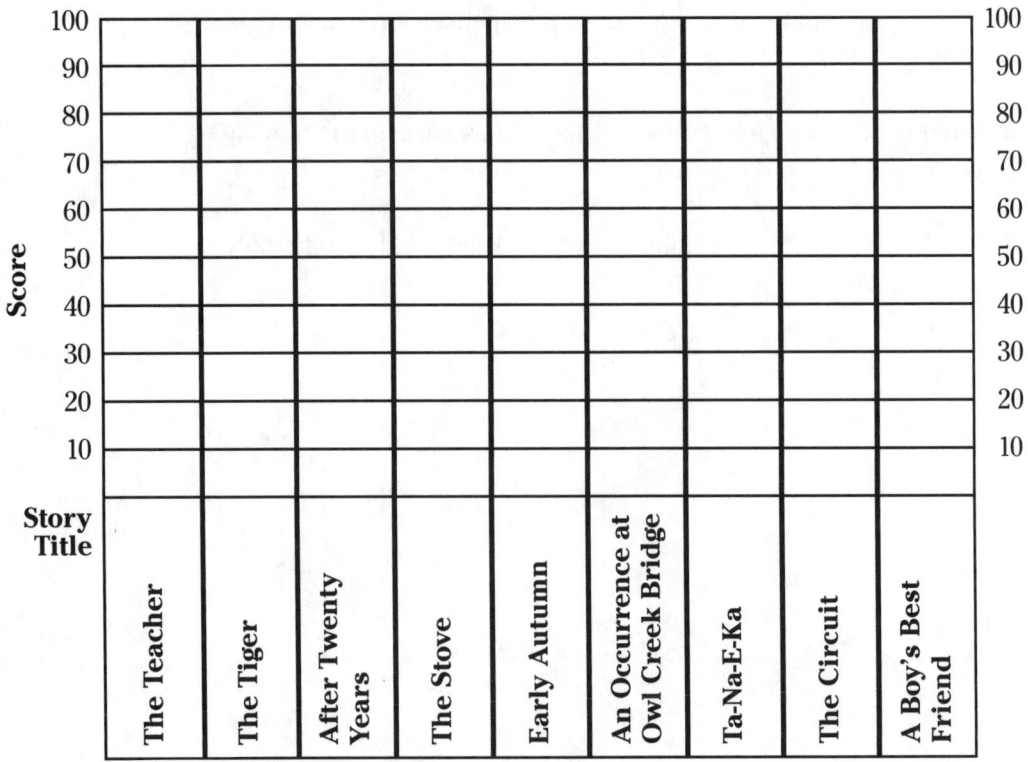